CATECHIZING
OUR CHILDREN

CATECHIZING OUR CHILDREN

The Hows and Whys of Teaching
the *Shorter Catechism* Today

Terry L. Johnson

THE BANNER OF TRUTH TRUST

THE BANNER OF TRUTH TRUST

3 Murrayfield Road, Edinburgh EH12 6EL, UK
P.O. Box 621, Carlisle, PA 17013, USA

*

© Terry L. Johnson 2013
First published 2013
Reprinted 2016

ISBN:
Print: 978 1 84871 300 0
EPUB: 978 1 84871 301 7
Kindle: 978 1 84871 302 4

*

Typeset in 10/13 pt Sabon Oldstyle Figures
at the Banner of Truth Trust, Edinburgh

Printed in the USA by
Versa Press, Inc.,
East Peoria, IL

CONTENTS

Introduction   vii

1. Environment   1
2. History   7
3. Strengths   17
4. Structure   29
5. Programme   63

Bibliographies & Charts   75

INTRODUCTION

EVANGELICAL ministry, such as it is, to a significant degree
has failed in our day. Regarding theology itself, the
Pew Forum on Religion and Public Life reports widespread
biblical ignorance and theological heterodoxy. For example,
52 per cent of evangelicals believe that salvation is possible
apart from Jesus, prompting Albert Mohler, President of
Southern Baptist Theological Seminary, Louisville, to claim,
'We are witnessing a virtual collapse of evangelical theology.' He sees as well in the survey results 'an indictment of
evangelicalism and evangelical preaching.'

'Moralistic Therapeutic Deism' is the label that has
been used by researchers to describe the beliefs of American teenagers. Christian Smith and his fellow scholars at
the National Study of Youth & Religion at the University
of North Carolina call this 'the actual dominant religion
among U.S. teenagers.' This faith commitment, they explain,
'is centrally about feeling good.'

This 'dominant religion' has infected the church. Surveys of the beliefs and morals of evangelical youth and young adults, conducted by the Barna Group and others, are discouraging, to say the least. Doctrinal and moral relativism are rampant, doctrinal and ethical ignorance pervasive. Promiscuity by evangelical adolescents and young adults is widespread. Indeed, if the surveys are to be believed, they are abandoning the church, if not the faith, in massive numbers, 'Quitting Church,' according to the title of one recent publication.

How, then, are we to transmit our faith, both its content and vitality, to our children? This is not a new question. The Bible does not hide the bad examples of Adam's Cain (Gen. 4:3ff), Aaron's Nadab and Abihu (*Lev.* 10:1, 2), Eli's sons (*1 Sam.* 2:12-17; 22-25), Samuel's sons (*1 Sam.* 8:1-6), David's Amnon and Absalom (*2 Sam.* 13), Hezekiah's Manasseh (*2 Kings* 21:2ff), Josiah's Jehoahaz (*2 Kings* 23:32), and the prodigal son of Jesus' parable (*Luke* 15:11ff). Godly families have not infrequently produced ungodly children.

On the other hand, we have the promise of God: I will be God to you 'and to your offspring after you' (*Gen.* 17:7). This is the promise of the covenant, the promise of circumcision and baptism, the same promise repeated by Peter in his Pentecost sermon (*Acts* 2:39). The children of believers 'are,' not 'might be,' not 'eventually will be,' but are 'holy' (*1 Cor.* 7:14). The baptismal waters pouring over our infants represent the promise of God to wash, regenerate, and sanctify our children (*Titus* 3:5). Adam also had an Abel and a Seth, Aaron had an Eleazar and an Ithamar, David had a Solomon, Hezekiah's grandson was Josiah, and the prodigal son, in the end, came home.

Testimonies from the past encourage us about the faith of children brought up in Christian homes. We think of the Bonar family in Scotland. Horatius Bonar (1808–1889) wrote a number of our hymns. His brother Andrew (1810–92) edited *The Memoir and Remains of Robert Murray M'Cheyne*. Both wrote outstanding books still in use today. All four of the Bonar brothers became ministers. They represented the fifth consecutive generation of Scottish Presbyterian ministers. We have heard it said (though we cannot confirm it) that there were eight successive generations of Bonars in the ministry.

Consider the Mather family in New England. Richard Mather (1596–1669), the immigrant, was one of the compilers of the *Bay Psalm Book*, and a drafter of *The Cambridge Platform* (1648) of church government. He sired Increase (1629–1723). Increase wrote 130 books and pamphlets, and served as president of Harvard for sixteen years. He married a daughter of John Cotton (that the daughters of clergy marry clergy is a well-established pattern), another of New England's founding pastors, and they gave birth to Cotton (1663–1728), who wrote over 400 books and was a member of the prestigious Royal Society. Cotton fathered several sons who followed him into the ministry, and on the ministerial line continued, until it died out with another minister, his grandson, the Rev. Samuel Mather (1706–1785). Mathers were in New England pulpits for over 150 years.

The same impact can be shown for the family of Archibald Alexander (1772–1851), founder of Princeton Seminary, and his brilliant sons J. A. Alexander (1809–1860) and J. W. Alexander (1804–1859), both ministers and Princeton theologians. Great-grandson Maitland Alexander (1867–1940), son of Henry M. Alexander, served as pastor and pastor emeritus of First Presbyterian Church, Pittsburgh, from 1899–1940, and served Princeton Seminary as President of its Board of Directors from 1904 until its reorganization in 1929. The Alexanders served Bible-believing Presbyterianism in America from Archibald's licensure in 1791 until Maitland's death in 1940, a total of nearly 150 years, four generations of ministers, from the presidency of George Washington to that of Franklin D. Roosevelt.

Charles Hodge (1797–1878), the greatest of America's nineteenth century theologians, sired Archibald Alexander Hodge (1823–1886), missionary and theologian, and C. W. Hodge (1830–1891), who in turn reared Caspar Wistar Hodge, Jr. (1870–1937), who continued the Hodge family's presence on the faculty of Old Princeton into the late 1930s. From the Administration of President James Monroe to that of Franklin Roosevelt there was a Hodge teaching theology at Princeton. A major new biography of Charles Hodge identifies his mother's method of instruction. 'She regularly brought Hodge and his older brother to her pastor, Ashbel Green, to be drilled in the memorization and recitation of the *Westminster Shorter Catechism*.' Paul C. Gutjahr, the author, claims that, 'Mastery of the catechism was central to Hodge's early theological development . . . the doctrines he memorized as a boy provided the foundation for the theological views he held his entire life.'

Perhaps the most outstanding Christian home in American history was that of Jonathan Edwards (1703–1758). Edwards' maternal grandfather was the famous 'Pope of the Connecticut Valley,' Solomon Stoddard, who for nearly 60 years (1672–1729) was the pastor of the Northampton

Church in which Edwards would serve as his successor. His father, Timothy Edwards (1669–1759) was a graduate of Harvard and a minister in New England. Jonathan's wife, Sarah Pierpoint, was the daughter of a New England minister (as was her mother) and a great granddaughter of the Rev. Thomas Hooker, founder of the Connecticut colony and among the most renowned of the first generation of Puritan ministers. Jonathan and Sarah's son, Jonathan Edwards Jr. (1745–1801), followed his father into the ministry, and their grandson, the Rev. Timothy Dwight (1752–1817), was a leader of the Second Great Awakening, President of Yale, and one of the outstanding clergymen of the late eighteenth or early nineteenth centuries. According to Elisabeth Dodds in her delightful book, *Marriage to a Difficult Man*, by 1900 one hundred descendants of Jonathan and Sarah had served overseas as missionaries and 'they had entered the ministry in platoons.' Thirteen had become college presidents and dozens had served society as judges and statesmen, professors, and doctors. These examples from the past of devout homes could be multiplied a thousand times over.

Let us cite a more recent example. Halvar Iverson was a port missionary, running the Seaman's Bethel in Savannah, Georgia in the 1890s. His son, Daniel (1890-1977) dated his call to the ministry to the occasion when, as a 7-year-old boy, he heard the great D. L. Moody (1837–1899) preach at the historic Independent Presbyterian Church of Savannah. For decades Daniel served as the minister of the Shenandoah Presbyterian Church in Miami, Florida. God used Daniel to plant 21 Presbyterian churches and send 150 ministers and missionaries around the world. His son, William (b.

1928), followed his father into the Presbyterian ministry, in which he has served for 6 decades. His daughter, Lalla, was a PCUS medical missionary to China and India. William's son, Daniel (b. 1952), who also was ordained, has served as a missionary in Japan for over 25 years. Daniel's son, Jonathan (b. 1979), was ordained as a Presbyterian minister in 2010, and is currently serving with his wife Maggie as a missionary in India.

Godly homes, lay and clergy, are effective nurseries for Christian disciples because of the promises of the covenant: God is faithful to his covenant to the thousandth generation of those who love him and keep his commandments (*Deut.* 7:9). The Christian home has been the most effective instrument of soul-winning and disciple-making in the history of the church. God uses devout homes to save, sanctify, and render serviceable his people, and to build his church.

Christian parents are caught between the bad boys of the Bible and the promises of God. Our faith can be transmitted to our children but, clearly, the process is not automatic. Faithful parents will continue to be challenged by prodigal children. A godly generation may be followed by another generation who '[do] not know the LORD, or the work that he [has] done for Israel' (*Judg.* 2:10). Sadly godly lines come to an end. Eventually spiritual movements lose momentum. Children who lack the ardour of their parents are born to zealous families.

Still, we may be encouraged. Most typically faith is passed from parents to children by the faithful use of means. Devout parents who will read the Bible to their children, who will pray with and for them, and who will take them to the public services of the church can hope for positive results. We note as well that the children in every single one of the above families, without exception, cut their teeth on the *Shorter Catechism*. It has been, over the decades, in conjunction with authentic piety, prayer, and Scripture reading, the most effective means of transmitting the faith to children that Reformed Protestantism has known. It has served as Calvinism's gospel tract, as we will argue. We are writing to urge its use. However, before we can discuss catechizing our children we must further discuss, however briefly, the context in which catechizing takes place. The catechism does not function *ex opere operato*. Effective catechizing requires an environment, specifically the two-fold environment of family and church, for it to bear fruit in our children's lives.

Terry L. Johnson
July 2013

ENVIRONMENT

E DUCATORS in recent years have come to recognize what pastors have observed for generations: parents are the primary teachers, for good or ill, of their children. Put another way, it is exceedingly difficult for secondary institutions (like the church and school) to overcome the deficiencies of the home environment, or even undo the assets of a positive home environment. The parents, in the end, win.

Christian home

What, then, is the context within which catechizing is to occur if it is to have its optimum sanctifying impact? *First, the well–ordered Christian home* is the foundation upon which is built the discipleship of covenant children in the 'discipline and instruction' (NASB, ESV), what the old version termed the 'nurture and admonition of the Lord' (*Eph.* 6:4 KJV). Fathers are charged with this responsibility. The promise regarding Abraham's children in Genesis 17:7 was followed by the instruction of Genesis 18:19, that he should 'command his children and his household after him to keep the way of the LORD by doing righteousness and justice, *so that the LORD may bring to Abraham what he has promised him.*'[1] The gracious promises of God are fulfilled through the faithful use of means, through Abraham instructing his children respecting the 'way of the LORD' in 'righteousness' and 'justice'.

Similarly, Moses, when laying the foundation for the life of the people of God in the soon-to-be-entered Promised Land, insisted upon the same, clearly addressing parents in what Douglas Kelly termed the *locus classicus* of parental responsibility for the spiritual nurture of children:[2]

> And these words that I command you today shall be on your heart. You shall teach them diligently to your children, and shall talk of them when you sit in your house, and when you walk by the way, and when you lie down, and when you rise. You shall bind them as a sign on your hand, and they shall be as frontlets between your eyes. You shall write them on the doorposts of your house and on your gates (*Deut.* 6:6–9; cf. 4:9, 10; 11:18–19; 28:4).

'You (parents) shall teach them diligently to your sons

[1] My emphasis.
[2] Douglas F. Kelly, 'The Westminster Shorter Catechism,' in John L. Carson and David W. Hall (eds.) *To Glorify & Enjoy God: A Commemoration of the 350th Anniversary of the Westminster Assembly* (Edinburgh: The Banner of Truth Trust, 1994), p. 103.

(children).' The question and answer teaching format may even be seen in Deuteronomy 6:20–25 regarding the commandments of God: 'When your son asks you . . . then you shall say . . .' and prior to this in Exodus 12:26–27, regarding the Passover:

> And when your children say to you, 'What do you mean by this service?' you shall say, 'It is the sacrifice of the LORD's Passover, for he passed over the houses of the people of Israel in Egypt, when he struck the Egyptians but spared our houses.' And the people bowed their heads and worshipped (cf. *Exod.* 13:14).

Parents teach; children ask questions; parents provide answers. Givens B. Strickler (1840–1913), the nineteenth century Southern Presbyterian pastor and Professor of Systematic Theology at Union Theological Seminary in Virginia, explained the implication of these passages. 'In these instances,' he argued, 'in order to give children the full and accurate instruction they needed about the commandments of the Lord referred to, and about the important sacrament instituted in the church in the Passover, it was necessary that a number of questions should be asked and answered.'[3] This was the regular means of education *then*; catechizing today merely formalizes this ancient method *now*. The questions sprinkled throughout the psalms (e.g. *Psa.* 42, 120, 121), as well as antiphonal elements of call and response (e.g. *Psa.* 122–134) may also suggest what Kelly calls a 'catechetical

[3] Givens Strickler, 'The Nature, Value, and Specific Utility of the Catechisms,' in Francis Beattie, Charles Hemphill, and Henry Escott (eds.), *Memorial Volume of the Westminster Assembly, 1647–1897* (Richmond, VA: The Presbyterian Committee of Publication, 1897), p. 117.

rubric.'[4] Divine truth was to be taught, meditated upon, and memorized (*Psa.* 1:2; 119:11). 'You shall therefore lay up these words of mine in your heart and in your soul,' (*Deut.* 11:18). No dichotomy between head and heart is contemplated. The head (teaching) was rather the means to the heart (devotion).

Parental *teaching* coupled with parental *example* are indispensable, and while not infallible, yet are powerful means of sanctifying the children born into Christian homes. What is taught must also be lived. Children must grow up seeing parents practising devotion to God (i.e. private devotional practices), commitment to Christ and his church (i.e. attendance and service), ethical precision, and love of neighbour, including a burden for lost souls. Without the daily domestic example of Christian lives being lived with integrity, we have little hope of catechetical usefulness.

Parental teaching and example, integrated in the discipline of daily family worship, has an important role to play. The daily sacrifices of the temple are to be mirrored by the devotional practices of the people of God, Old Testament and New Testament (see *Psa.* 141:1–2). Daily prayers, songs, and Scripture reading in the home are vital if our faith is to be passed on to our children.[5]

Church

Second, in addition to the well–ordered home, *the well– ordered church* is also foundational for the proper nurture of Christian children. Effective catechical instruction is built

---

[4] Kelly, 'Shorter Catechism,' p. 103.

[5] See Johnson, *The Family Worship Book* (Fearn, Ross–shire: Christian Focus Publications, 2003).

on both the 'family altar,' that is, family devotions, and on the 'family pew,' as the family worshipping together in the public services of the church has been called. A commitment to the church's public services places the children of the covenant under the ministry of the Word, Sunday morning and evening, week in and week out, year after year, all through their childhood and youth. A 'well-ordered' church is one in which worship is God-centred, Word-filled, gospel-shaped, prayer-dependent, and demographically diverse (i.e. it is catholic, in the best sense of that word). Children grow up hearing the Word read, preached, sung, prayed, and administered in the sacraments. What is taught in the catechism is reinforced weekly in the church's public services and in its Sunday School. The truth preached underscores truth taught in the catechism, and vice versa. Devotion seen and expressed in public worship reinforces devotion expressed in the catechism.

God certainly can use the catechizing in a vacuum, without the supports of family and church. However, we would guess that this is rare. The catechism requires a context, an environment, and that environment is the well-ordered family and the well-ordered church. Given this context, the people of God, through the centuries, have found catechizing to be an effective means of transmitting the content of the gospel to their children, and more broadly, to those in need of instruction. The use of the catechism will not eliminate the problem of prodigals. However, we do believe that its faithful use may minimize the likelihood of any given child going astray.

2

HISTORY

CATECHISM is a biblical term. It is taken from the Greek word *katēchein*, which means to instruct orally.

> . . . it seemed good to me also, having followed all things closely for some time past, to write an orderly account for you, most excellent Theophilus, that you may have certainty concerning the things you have been taught (*Luke* 1:3–4).

Theophilus had been 'taught' (*katēcheō*); Luke was now to 'write it out' (cf. *1 Cor.* 14:19). The early Christians used the term to indicate both the pedagogical process (teaching method) and the content (what was taught). Beginning in the earliest centuries, converts were given extensive instruction in preparation for baptism (adult converts) and/or first communion (those baptized in infancy). They were called catechumen. Eventually the books containing the instruction given to catechumens came to be called catechisms. Early examples include Cyril of Jerusalem's *Catechetical Lectures* (c. 350), Gregory of Nyssa's *Catechetical Oration* (late fourth century), and Augustine's *On the Catechizing of the Uninstructed* (c. 400), and his *Enchiridion* (423). Augustine seems to have been the first to recommend that the Ten Commandments be taught to catechumens along with the Lord's Prayer and the Apostles' Creed, which were standardized earlier. These three 'pattern(s) of sound words' became the core of all future catechetical instruction (2 *Tim.* 1:13). Catechesis is an ancient and honoured practice of the church.

The Middle Ages were once thought to be devoid of catechetical teaching. However, scholars have brought to light a number of medieval catechisms, and catechetical sermons are known to have been preached regularly. After the invention of the printing press around 1450, a number of catechisms for lay people began to be published, including those for children. The Reformation, because it placed emphasis on both the instruction of the young and the laity, brought about a flurry of catechetical activity. Luther's first attempts at catechesis began as early as 1516 or 1517. His preaching and writing through the mid-1520s urged catechetical instruction. Denis R. Janz, writing in *The Oxford Encyclopedia of the Reformation*, explains:

> He directed all of this material first and foremost to the heads of households, who, he held, had the primary responsibility for 'impressing' or 'imprinting' (*einbilden*) these basic Christian truths on the minds of the young through memorization and frequent repetition.[1]

[1] Denis R. Janz, 'Catechisms', in *The Oxford Encyclopedia of the*

His emphasis would later shift, as was so often the case, yet his thinking would prove influential as others would seize his seminal ideas and develop them—memorization and frequent repetition in particular. Luther produced two catechisms in 1529, following his visitation to the churches in Saxony which uncovered what he described as appalling ignorance: a *Deutsch Catechismus*, hereafter known as the Larger or Greater Catechism, and *Der Kleine Catechismus*, the Small Catechism.[2] Following the historic pattern, both included expositions of the Lord's Prayer, Apostles' Creed, and the Ten Commandments, though he altered the medieval order, his catechisms moving successively from Law (which, says Luther, 'shows man his disease'), to the Creed (which, he continues, 'tells him where to find his medicine'), and then the Lord's Prayer (which, he concludes, 'teaches him how to seek it and appropriate it'). Luther's gospel determines the arrangement of his catechism. It is a Pauline order, the order of Romans. The catechisms also treat the sacraments, among other things, and the *Small Catechism* in particular proved to be a huge success. Luther's catechisms helped to spread and consolidate the Reformation in Europe.[3]

Among Reformed Protestants, early catechisms were written by Oecolampadius (1482–1531) in Basel, Leo Jud (1482–1542) in Zurich, Wolgang Capito (1478–1541) and Martin Bucer (1491–1551) in Strasbourg, and Pierre Viret (1511–1571) in Lausanne. However, the most important

---

Reformation, Vol. 1, Hans J. Hillerbrand, Ed. (New York, NY: Oxford University Press, 1996), p. 276.

[2] Ibid.

[3] Ibid., p. 277.

of Reformed catechisms was Calvin's for children, known as the *Genevan Catechism*, first published in 1537, then heavily revised in 1542. It featured the question and answer format and follows the familiar outline of the Apostles' Creed, the Ten Commandments, and the Lord's Prayer, concluding with the sacraments. It quickly became the preferred catechism among Reformed Protestants, replacing even Heinrich Bullinger's (1504–1575), and remained dominant until superseded by the Heidelberg Catechism in 1563. From the beginning of his pastoral charge in Geneva in 1537, and reaffirmed in his *Ecclesiastical Ordinance* in 1541, Calvin insisted on reviving the ancient practice of catechetical instruction, establishing a midday Sunday catechism class for children.

At the behest of Elector Frederick III of the Palatinate, two Reformed theologians at the University of Heidelberg, Casper Olevianus (1536–1587) and Zacharius Ursinus (1534–1583), completed a new catechism in 1563, named for the town and University in which it was written. Consisting of 129 questions divided into 52 sections (so as to facilitate yearly catechetical preaching), the Heidelberg Catechism became the most widely used catechism of the sixteenth century, and is still today the standard for Dutch and German Reformed churches. It is best known for its beautiful opening question:

Q 1: What is your only comfort in life and death?

A: That I am not my own, but belong—body and soul, in life and in death—to my faithful Saviour Jesus Christ. He has fully paid for all my sins with his precious blood, and has set me free from the tyranny of the devil. He also watches over me in such a way that not a hair can fall from my head without the will of my Father in heaven: in fact, all things must work together for my salvation. Because I belong to him, Christ, by his Holy Spirit, assures me of eternal life and makes me wholeheartedly willing and ready from now on to live for him.

In the English-speaking world, Thomas Cranmer provided a catechism in the first *Book of Common Prayer* (1549). Over time others were developed, such as John Ponet's *A Shorter Catechism* (1553) and Alexander Nowell's *A Catechism* (1570). In Scotland John Craig's *Catechism* of 1581 came into widespread use, as well as his *Shorter Catechism* (1592), an abridgement of the former, and was used in the examination of young people prior to admission to the Lord's Table. Another attempt was made by the Scottish church to produce a catechism truly suitable for young children, resulting in the publishing of *The A,B,C or A Catechism for Young Children* in 1641. 'It went through several editions,' explains T. F. Torrance, 'before the *Shorter Catechism* took the field and swept everything before it.'[4] The influence of the latter, according to David C. Lachman, would be 'difficult to overestimate.'[5] Following its publication in 1648, it became the most widely used catechism in the English-speaking world.

Still, because the Westminster Assembly's *Shorter Catechism* was not suitable for younger children, a number of

---

[4] Thomas F. Torrance, *The School of Faith* (New York, NY: Harper & Brothers Publishers, 1959), p. 255.

[5] D. C. Lachman, 'Catechisms (English & Scots)' in *Dictionary of Scottish Church History & Theology* (Downers Grove, IL: InterVarsity Press, 1993), p. 142.

attempts were made to write a simpler catechism, or sup-plement the *Shorter* with a series of subordinate questions. Richard Baxter (1615–1691), Matthew Henry (1662–1714), and John Willison (1680–1750) wrote the former (see below), while noted Puritans such as Joseph Alleine (1633–1668), Hugh Binning (d. 1653), Thomas Vincent (d. 1671), and John Flavel (1627–1691) are examples of the latter, as well as James Fisher's *The Assembly's Shorter Catechism Explained* (1753), and John Brown of Haddington's (1751–1787) *Easy Explication.*[6] Full theological systems based on the *Shorter Catechism* were written by Thomas Watson (*A Body of Practical Divinity*, 1692), Thomas Doolitte (d. 1707) (*A Complete Body of Divinity*), New Englanders Samuel Willard (1640-1707) and Ashbel Green (d. 1848), the Scot Thomas Boston (1773), and others. The same trend continued throughout the nineteenth century, supplementing and/or elaborating upon the *Shorter Catechism*.[7]

Beyond the *Shorter Catechism*, many Reformed Protestants wrote their own catechisms. For example, John Owen wrote two catechisms in 1645, *The Lesser Catechism* for children consisting of 32 questions, and *The Greater Catechism* with 142 questions for adults.

Richard Baxter (1615–1691) commends the Westminster Assembly's *Shorter Catechism* in the strongest terms, yet also offered the church *The Poor Man's Family Book* in

---

[6] Flavel and Vincent remain in print. See John Flavel, 'An Exposition of the Assembly's Shorter Catechism with Practical Inferences from Each Question,' in *The Works of John Flavel, Vol. 6* (1820; reprinted Edinburgh: The Banner of Truth Trust, 1968), 138-317; and Thomas Vincent, *The Shorter Catechism Explained from Scripture* (1674; reprinted Edinburgh: The Banner of Truth Trust, 1980).

[7] See the bibliographies for some of these.

1672, which contained two catechisms, 'The Shortest Catechism,' and a longer 'A Short Catechism,' for those who had learned the first. He wrote a third, *The Catechizing of Families*, in 1682, which explained the Creed, the Ten Commandments, and the sacraments, and a fourth, *The Mother's Catechism*, which death prevented him from finishing.[8]

Similarly, Matthew Henry (1662–1714) provides not only an exposition of the *Shorter Catechism* through subordinate questions that runs to 83 pages in his *Works*, entitled *A Scripture Catechism, in the Method of the Assembly*, but also published *A Plain Catechism for Children* in 1703, designed to prepare young children for the *Shorter Catechism*, consisting of sixty-seven short answer questions. This was followed by *A Short Catechism* of thirty questions concerning the Lord's Supper. He also preached 'A Sermon Concerning the Catechizing of Youth; Preached to Mr. Harris' Catechumens, April 7, 1713.'[9]

We trust that we have shown that the practice of catechizing is deeply rooted in the history of the church and received particular commitment in the Reformed tradition. Givens Strickler sums up our case in arguing that, 'Teaching, by the catechetical method, has marked the history of the church almost from the beginning down to the present time.'[10] So successful were the Reformers in their catechetical labours that the Roman Catholics honoured them

[8] All of these are found in Richard Baxter, *The Practical Works of Richard Baxter, Vol. IV* (19th century; reprinted Ligonier, PA: Soli Deo Gloria, 1990-91).

[9] All of these are found in Matthew Henry, *The Complete Works of Matthew Henry*, Vol. II (1855; Grand Rapids, MI: Baker Book House, 1979).

[10] Strickler, 'Nature, Value of Catechisms,' p. 117.

with the flattery of imitation, producing their own. One of the ironies of the late twentieth and early twenty-first centuries is that catechizing is now often associated in the popular mind with Roman Catholics, when in fact it was originally a Protestant reform. The list of those who have written catechisms or have written books explaining the catechisms reads like a 'who's who' of Reformed pastors and theologians. The very best of the heritage of Reformed Protestantism is devoted to catechizing as an indispensable means by which to transmit the content of the Reformed faith to the children of the Reformed church. From Augustine to Luther to Calvin to the Puritans to Matthew Henry to eighteenth and nineteenth century Reformed orthodoxy, catechizing receives enthusiastic endorsement. John Owen (1616–1683), perhaps the greatest of English theologians, summarizes the outlook of the Reformed Church: 'after the ordinance of public preaching of the Word, there is not, I conceive, any more needful (ordinance) . . . than catechizing.'[11] To the list of advocates we can add the name of J. I. Packer, who with Gary A. Parrett, recently called the church back to serious catechesis.[12] They endorse Calvin's stern warning to the Lord Protector of England: 'Believe me, Monsignor, the Church of God will never be preserved without catechesis.'[13] The great Puritan Thomas Watson (c. 1620–1686) sounds a similar warning:

[11] John Owen, *The Works of John Owen*, ed. William H. Goold (1850-53; Edinburgh: The Banner of Truth Trust, 1965), Vol. 1, 465.
[12] J. I. Packer and Gary A. Parrett, *Grounded in the Gospel: Building Believers in the Old-Fashioned Way* (Grand Rapids, MI: Baker Books, 2010).
[13] Ibid., p. 23.

I fear one reason why there has been no more good done by preaching, has been because the chief heads and articles in religion have not been explained in a catechetical way . . . To preach and not to catechize is to build without foundation.[14]

Be very slow, very slow indeed, to ignore so great a cloud of witnesses.

[14] Thomas Watson, *A Body of Divinity*, (1692, reprinted London: The Banner of Truth Trust, 1965), p. 5.

3

STRENGTHS

THE quality of the men gathered at the Westminster Assembly (1643–1648), pastors and theologians, is perhaps without parallel in the history of the church. Richard Baxter considered it the greatest gathering of divines since the days of the apostles. Puritan luminaries such as Thomas Manton, Thomas Goodwin, William Gouge, Thomas Gatlaker, Edward Reynolds, Jeremiah Burroughs, Stephen Marshall, and the Scotsmen, Samuel Rutherford and George Gillespie, among others, carried out the Assembly's work. It is not surprising, given the foregoing history, that twelve to fourteen members of the Westminster Assembly which would produce the *Shorter Catechism* had already written their own catechisms. Following the completion of the *Confession of Faith* (1645), the Assembly produced two catechisms, the *Larger* based on the Confession, and the *Shorter* based on the *Larger*, both approved in final form in 1648. The *Shorter* was the fruit of five years of careful, painstaking work by men eminently qualified for the task. Strickler explains the labour of the four committees that worked on it, concluding, 'Not a sentence was admitted into them until after the most protracted and thorough consideration. Not a word was allowed a place in them until it had been subjected to the closest scrutiny, and had proved itself to be just the right word to express the meaning intended.'[1] T. F. Torrance (1913–2007), often critical of the Assembly's work, calls the *Shorter* 'one of the greatest and most remarkable documents in the whole history of Christian theology.'[2] 'At once,' he says, it became 'the most popular and widely used Catechism in Scotland as in England.'[3] To them we can add North America as well.

What are the strengths of the *Shorter Catechism* that propelled it to pre–eminence among catechisms in the English–speaking world? We may identify the following.

Evangelistic

The *Shorter Catechism* is designed to lead the church's children to Christ. Its order is that of the gospel, even of the book of Romans, moving from the God who is to be glorified and enjoyed (Qs 1–11), to a ruined humanity (Qs 12–19), to God's gracious provision of salvation through a Redeemer (Qs 20–28). This salvation is planned by the Father (Q 20), accomplished through the Son (Qs 21–28), whose work as prophet, priest, and king is the heart of the catechism. The Holy Spirit is identified as the agent of

---

[1] Strickler, 'Nature, Value of Catechisms,' p. 130.
[2] Torrance, *School of Faith*, p. 262.
[3] Ibid.

application, the Spirit regenerating the sinner and making possible the faith and repentance by which justification, adoption, sanctification, perseverance, and glorification are possible, as well as the assurance, peace, and joy that flow from them (Qs 29–38).

The catechism gives the law of God substantial attention. However, it does so only once it has established that salvation is *solo Christo*, *sola fide*, *sola gratia*. Only then does it move on to the law of God (Qs 39–84) and the duties of the Christian life (Qs 85–107). These only come into view once the *ordo salutis* has been established, from election to glorification. As we shall demonstrate more thoroughly in later sections, the *Shorter Catechism* is best understood as a comprehensive gospel tract, designed to lead our children to Christ, and then to the life that is ours in Christ.

Pedagogy

The question and answer format, what secular education calls the 'Socratic' method, and what we have suggested is a 'Mosaic' and 'Davidic' method, is an excellent approach to instruction. It has a number of advantages over other formats.

First, it focuses attention sharply on the subject. It is specific – 'what is sin?'; 'what is saving faith?'; 'who is the Redeemer of God's elect?'

Second, as it focuses attention, it immediately uncovers what the student does and doesn't know. It forces the student to search for words with which to provide the answer and then supplies the student with an accurate answer. 'This mode of teaching,' says Strickler, has resting upon it the unqualified endorsement of the church in all ages, especially in her best ages; and that it has been one of the most efficient of all the agencies which God has made use of to secure those blessed results by which the past history of the church has been marked.[4]

Comprehensiveness

The *Shorter Catechism* provides a comprehensive summary of Christian theology. Let us say as carefully as we are able: it is not enough to study the Bible. The Bible is the sourcebook for our doctrine. However, the Bible never gathers together what it teaches on a given subject and gives it a succinct and comprehensive expression. That task is left to us. Can we speak of what the Bible, not just the Old Testament, and not just the New Testament, and not just Moses or David or Paul or James, but the whole Bible has to say about God, creation, man, sin, salvation, Christian living, and the end times? One of the problems the conservative, evangelical church has today is that its members, its youth in particular, have had bits and pieces of Bible from time to time, but the doctrine of the Bible as a whole has not been taught. Our youth are vulnerable to secularism and the cults because they do not know what the Bible teaches about the Trinity, about the dual nature of Christ, about the fall, about the nature and extent of the atonement, about justification and sanctification, about the means of grace, or the end times. They are vulnerable not only to the cults and secularists, but to the charismatics, the dispensationalists,

---

[4] Strickler, 'Nature, Value of Catechisms', p. 122.

the Adventists, the theonomists, the 'New Perspective on Paul,' legalists, antinomians, and name what one will.

The catechism is a valuable tool because it covers the whole range of Christian doctrine. Yet, it is more than a mere compilation of *doctrine*, providing a comprehensive guide to *ethics* as well. It teaches both 'what man is to believe concerning God' and 'what duty God requires of man.' It lays 'a foundation of doctrine,' as John F. Cannon says in the same *Memorial Volume* mentioned earlier, and then proceeds to 'rear upon it a superstructure of duty.'[5] Nearly half of the *Shorter Catechism* is devoted to ethics. Ron Gleason, in a recent paper, calls it 'a veritable treasure trove of practical Christian living.'[6] The single exception to the claim of comprehensiveness is the doctrine of the church, which according to W. Robert Godfrey, is 'almost entirely absent.'[7] One may turn to the *Larger Catechism* to supplement this lack, drawing on such questions as numbers 61–65. For example,

Q 62: What is the visible church?

A: The visible church is a society made up of all such as in all ages and places of the world do profess the true religion, and of their children.

Q 64: What is the invisible church?

---

[5] John F. Cannon, 'The Influence Exerted by the Westminster Symbols upon the Individuals, the Family, and Society,' in Beattie, Hemphill, and Escott (eds.), *Memorial Volume,* p. 261.

[6] Ron Gleason, unpublished paper, 'A 21st Century Plea for Catechizing Our Covenant Children,' July 2011, p. 22.

[7] W. Robert Godfrey, 'The Westminster Larger Catechism,' in Carson & Hall (eds.) *To Glorify & Enjoy God*, p. 34.

A: The invisible church is the whole number of the elect, that have been, are, or shall be gathered into one under Christ the head.

This exception noted, the *Shorter Catechism* provides an impressively complete summary of Christian doctrine. 'By these forms of sound words,' said Matthew Henry of the catechism, 'the main principles of Christianity, which lie scattered in Scripture, are collected and brought together.'[8] The result: 'Those who are well catechized, are well fortified against temptations to atheism and infidelity,' and have as well, he says, 'an excellent antidote against the poison of popery.'[9]

Logical Order

The *Shorter Catechism* presents the major themes of Christian doctrine in a logical, coherent order. 'The questions and answers have the conceptual order and beauty of a well–trained army,' says Kelly, 'marching in precise formation, one platoon following directly upon another in symmetrical and logical sequence.'[10] Following its matchless opening question, it moves logically from Scripture (the source of all the catechism's answers) to question number 3 which provides the catechism's two primary divisions: what man is to believe concerning God (Q 1–38) and what duty God requires of man (Q 39–107). We are introduced to God and his works, to man, to the fall and sin, to the Redeemer and

---

[8] Matthew Henry, 'A Sermon Concerning the Catechizing of Youth,' in *The Complete Works of the Rev. Matthew Henry in Two Volumes*, Vol. II, p. 160.

[9] Ibid., p. 164.

[10] Kelly, 'Shorter Catechism', p. 112.

his work, to the application of redemption (justification, adoption, etc.), that is, all that man is to believe concerning God. Then follows what duty God requires of man: the Ten Commandments, faith, repentance, and the means of grace (the Word, sacraments, and prayer), concluding with its exposition of the Lord's Prayer. It is beautifully, wonderfully logical. Its logic contributes rightly to its effectiveness and impact. Again we cite Henry:

> These forms of sound words show us the order that is in God's words, as well as in his works; the harmony of divine truths, how one thing tends to another, and all centre in Christ, and the glory of God in Christ: and thus, like the stones in an arch, they mutually support, and strengthen, and fix one another.[11]

It also has been suggested that memorizing logical, struc-tured, conceptual material like the *Shorter Catechism* actually contributes to mental development. J. S. Mill, no friend of orthodox Christianity, claimed in his famous essay, *On Liberty*, that the Scots had become mental philosophers of the first order through their study of the Bible and the *Shorter Catechism*. Douglas Kelly, noting the work of Scot-tish theologian T. F. Torrance, states that 'children brought up on the Catechism have a greater capacity for conceptual thinking (as opposed to merely pictorial thinking) than those who never memorized it.'[12] It provides matter (theological matter!) for building the mental framework within which rational thought can take place. While not superior to the memorization of Scripture, this does explain why the

[11] Henry, 'Sermon,' p. 161.
[12] Kelly, 'Shorter Catechism,' p. 124.

CATECHIZING OUR CHILDREN

Catechisms are to be memorized alongside of Scripture.

Conciseness

The fifth strength of the *Shorter Catechism* is succinctness and preciseness. Nineteenth century church historian Philip Schaff (1819–1893), comparing the *Shorter Catechism* to Luther's *Small Catechism* and the *Heidelberg Catechism*, claims 'it far surpasses them in clearness and careful wording,' and speaks of 'its concise and severely logical answers,' and 'its mathematical precision in definitions, some of which are almost perfect.'[13] He cites three examples:

Q 4: What is God?

A: God is a Spirit, infinite, eternal, and unchangeable, in His being, wisdom, power, holiness, justice, goodness, and truth.

Q 21:Who is the Redeemer of God's elect?

A: The only Redeemer of God's elect is the Lord Jesus Christ, who, being the eternal Son of God, became man, and so was, and continues to be, God and man in two distinct natures, and one person, for ever.

Q 92: What is a sacrament?

A: A sacrament is a holy ordinance instituted by Christ, wherein, by sensible signs, Christ, and the benefits of the new covenant, are represented, sealed, and applied to believers.

[13] Philip Schaff, *The Creeds of Christendom with a History and Critical Notes*, Vol. I, 'The History of Creeds' (1931, reprinted Grand Rapids, MI: Baker Book House, 1985), p. 787.

The great Princeton theologian, B. B. Warfield (1851–1921), made similar observations:

> No other Catechism can be compared with it in its concise, nervous, terse exactitude of definition, or in its severely logical elaboration; and it gains these admirable qualities at no expense to its freshness or fervour.[14]

The Apostle Paul speaks of the standard 'sound words' (*2 Tim.* 1:13), and the 'standard of teaching' to which the early Christians 'were committed' (*Rom.* 6:17). He may be referring exclusively to scriptural expressions, but this seems unlikely. Already the church was developing forms of words which summarized biblical teaching but exceeded the actual language of the Bible. This development would eventually result in creedal language like 'truly God and truly man,' 'one substance with the Father', 'holy catholic church', 'communion of saints', and doctrinal terminology like 'Trinity', 'communicable attributes', 'dual nature of Christ', 'original sin', 'substitutionary atonement', and 'sacrament', all of which exceed scriptural terminology. The church has developed this creedal and confessional language as shorthand for complex and sometimes difficult doctrines, as well as to give those doctrines succinct, accurate, precise expression.

The *Shorter Catechism's* brevity, answering the most profound of questions with the most concise of answers, makes it a serviceable aid to Christians for the rest of their lives. My son Andrew, when a junior at Wheaton College, was asked to write a paper evaluating the 'New Perspective

---

[14] Cited on the cover of the Banner of Truth Trust's first edition of the *Shorter Catechism*.

on Paul' with regard to justification. In order to evaluate the New Perspective he needed to identify the 'old perspective.' The traditional understanding was there on the tip of his tongue because of the *Shorter Catechism*:

> Q 33: What is Justification?
>
> A: Justification is an act of God's free grace, wherein He pardons all our sins, and accepts us as righteous in His sight, only for the righteousness of Christ imputed to us, and received by faith alone.

The catechism gave him his starting point for his analysis. What is God? What is sin? What is faith? What is repentance? What is prayer? What is man's chief end? These crucial themes receive concise, accurate expression in the *Shorter Catechism* to which our students can return again and again, for as long as they live. The great Scotsman of letters, Thomas Carlyle (1795–1881), made this confession in 1876:

> The older I grow—and I now stand upon the brink of eternity—the more comes back to me the first sentence in the Catechism which I learned when a child, and the fuller and deeper its meaning becomes: 'What is the chief end of man? To glorify God, and to enjoy him forever.'[15]

Biblical

From start to finish, from top to bottom, the *Shorter Catechism* is biblical. It summarizes from the Bible what we are to believe about God, and the duty which God requires

[15] Cited in Schaff, *Creeds of Christendom*, p. 787.

of us (Q 3). The aim of the catechism is not to add to or replace Scripture, rather, in the words of Matthew Henry, 'to collect and arrange the truths and laws of God, and to make them familiar.'[16] Nearly one–half of the catechism is straight biblical exposition: of the Ten Commandments (Qs 39–81) and the Lord's Prayer (Qs 99–107).

All 107 questions provide multiple 'Scripture proofs' where the given affirmation is taught. Those scriptural references have been treated with considerable condescension and scorn in recent decades, even by some from within the Reformed community. Recent scholarship, particularly that of Richard Muller, has demonstrated that the so–called 'proof texts' are rather 'sign-posts' pointing to an entire exegetical tradition that encompasses the best of patristic, medieval, and Reformed interpretation. Concurrent with the work of the Westminster Assembly the English Parliament authorized the compiling of the *English Annotations* (1645), the work of Thomas Gataker (1574-1654), a member of the Assembly, and others, covering the whole Bible in two volumes consisting of over 2400 folio pages in its final edition (1657). The *Annotations* are not direct explanations of the catechism's scriptural citations, but what Muller calls 'a highly proximate index to the understanding of Scripture behind the doctrinal definitions and the biblical proofs found in the confessions and catechisms.'[17] Moreover, Muller argues,

---

[16] Henry, 'Sermon', p. 160.

[17] Richard A. Muller, 'Scripture and the Westminster Confession,' in Richard A. Muller and Rowland S. Ward, *Scripture & Worship: Biblical Interpretation and the Directory for Public Worship* (Phillipsburg, NJ: P&R Publishing Co., 2007), p. 5.

[T]he pattern of citing biblical proofs found in the confessional standard was not a form of rank proof–texting, as has sometimes been alleged of the Westminster Standards and of the theological works of the seventeenth–century orthodox in general. Rather, the confession and the catechisms cite texts by way of referencing an exegetical tradition reaching back, in many cases, to the fathers of the church in the first five centuries of Christianity and, quite consistently, reflecting the path of biblical interpretation belonging to the Reformed tradition as it developed in the sixteenth century and in the beginning of the seventeenth.[18]

The *Shorter Catechism* represents the solid exegetical tradition of Reformed, catholic Protestantism.

Historic

The *Shorter Catechism* is historic. The format of questions and answers dates to the ancient baptismal rites of at least the fourth century A.D. and, as we have seen, perhaps as far back as Moses. The *Shorter Catechism* provides us with a tested form of words and a proven method of instruction. Multitudes of Protestant children have been taught the basic doctrines of Christian religion through the *Shorter Catechism*. Its recitation has been a rite of passage for generations. Educational fads come and go. Here is a method that has stood the test of time.

Evangelistically designed, pedagogically sound, logical, concise, biblical, historic: the *Shorter Catechism* is a valuable tool for parents who wish to pass on the contents of the Christian faith to their children.

[18] Ibid., p. 81.

4

STRUCTURE

Section 1: A Gospel–Driven Faith
(*Questions 1–38*)

As the Apostle Peter writes to the Christians of Asia Minor, he begins by unfolding for them the whole plan of salvation. He identifies them as 'those who are elect . . . according to the foreknowledge of God the Father' (*1 Pet.* 1:1b, 2). Their identity as Christians began, according to Peter, with the eternal purpose of God the Father to have a people. He identifies them further as those 'sprinkled with His blood' (NASB), that is, the blood of Jesus Christ, by whose death their salvation was accomplished (*1 Pet.* 1:2b). Finally, he identifies them as those set apart 'in the sanctification of the Spirit, for obedience to Jesus Christ,' or 'by the sanctifying work of the Spirit, that (they) may obey Jesus Christ' (*1 Pet.* 1:2, NASB). The apostle describes the saving work of God as a Trinitarian work, the Father *planning* redemption, the Son *accomplishing* redemption, and the Spirit *applying* it.

The apostle doesn't stop there. He then elaborates upon the details of redemption in 1 Peter 1:3–5: regeneration (the 'Father . . . caused us to be born again'), faith ('through faith', see also *1 Pet.* 1:7–9), perseverance ('who by God's power are being guarded'), and glorification ('an inheritance that is imperishable, undefiled, and unfading . . .'), adoption (*1 Pet.* 1:14–17 'as obedient children . . . call on him as Father'), are all identified, as was sanctification in verse 2. The apostle presents the whole gospel, from the Father's eternal plan to the believer's hope of heaven.[1]

Present the whole gospel is also what the *Shorter Catechism* does in Questions 1–38, in a way that is beautifully succinct and yet comprehensive. Those labouring to teach the catechism to their children may be encouraged to know that it is structured to present the *alpha* and *omega* of the gospel, each item in its proper place in the whole scheme of redemption, yet in a way that is logical and convincing. The *Shorter Catechism*, as we have suggested, is best understood as a gospel tract, moving relentlessly from God to man to Christ to the way of salvation.

God

The catechism begins with a transcendent and holy God (Qs 1–9, 11). No tradition has so high a view of God as Westminster Calvinism. He is utterly beyond us: 'infinite, eternal, and unchangeable' in all his being and attributes

---

[1] The Apostle Paul does much the same in Romans 8:12–30 and Ephesians 1:3ff.

(Q 4). He is the One God yet a trinity of persons who are 'the same in substance, equal in power and glory' (Q 6). Trinitarian orthodoxy, as formulated at Nicea (325) is affirmed. He is absolutely almighty and sovereign, decreeing 'whatsoever comes to pass' (Q 7). He has created all things, and he preserves and governs all things (Qs 8, 9, 11). He is present in all of creation, upholding and sustaining all things, yet distinguished from creation (*Acts* 17:28; *1 Kings* 8:27; *Jer.* 23:24).

Further, God condescends to us, revealing himself through his Word, the Old and New Testaments, which together are 'the only rule' by which we may know God and his will (Q 2). God is not only transcendent, above us and beyond us, he is also immanent, interacting with us. Two errors are hereby refuted: *deism*, the 'watchmaker' God, the God who is remote, removed, uninvolved in the creation; and the god of *pantheism*, the god who is pure immanence and indistinguishable from creation, for whom creation is an extension of the divine substance, meaning everything is god. The God of the Bible and the *Catechism* is both beyond us and near us, both almighty and personal, both holy and good.

This transcendent yet immanent God defines the whole purpose of our existence. The *Shorter Catechism* starts with God, the omniscient and omnipotent God, the just and wise God, as it should, doing what so much of contemporary Christianity fails to do, with its fixation on what is of interest to man, or helpful to man, or will benefit humanity. Why are we here? What is the reason for our existence, and the existence of all things? 'To glorify God and to enjoy Him forever' (Q 1).

Humanity

The *Shorter Catechism* next introduces a ruined humanity (Qs 10, 12–19); not that the human race started out that way. We are made 'after his own image,' the *Catechism* laying the foundation for our understanding of human dignity. We were created 'in righteousness and holiness', unfallen and uncorrupt (Q 10). Yet we were tested in the Garden of Eden (Q 12). The story of Genesis 3 is well known, and the *Catechism* repeats it (Qs 13, 15). Our first parents, functioning as representative humanity, failed their test. Sin, defined as 'any want of conformity unto or transgression of the law of God,' entered into the world, and brought ruin to all human posterity thereafter (Qs 14, 16). We note again the God–centredness: sin is defined in relation to God. Sin is not primarily harming my neighbour or even harming myself, it is 'against you, you only, have I sinned' (*Psa.* 51:4). The condition of humanity, notwithstanding the world's seductive images, the counterfeit and 'fleeting pleasures of sin' (*Heb.* 11:25), is one of *sin* and *misery* (Q 17). We have inherited guilt and corruption from Adam (Q 18). We are separated from God, subject to all the miseries of this life: sickness, pain, sorrow, natural disasters, conflict, alienation, crime, and war; we are under the wrath and curse of God, and death and hell await us (Q 19). Do not believe the lies of the devil, the flesh, and the world, the *Catechism* would warn us. They entice us with the promises of excitement, of perpetual pleasure and unending fun for all. However, what they is misery: superficial and temporary happiness, guilt, afflicted consciences, life without purpose, unfulfilled desires, a meaningless existence, and eternal damnation.

Redemption

No humanly–devised rescue for humanity is contemplated by Scripture or by the *Catechism*. If the human race is to be rescued it will have come from outside of itself. Beginning with Question 20 the source of that help is identified and the whole work unfolded through Question 38. How is humanity to be rescued from ruin? Only by *God's gracious provision*.

First, salvation begins with the Father's eternal plan. God, 'out of his mere good pleasure, from all eternity' determined to choose some for salvation, and save them from sin and misery 'by a Redeemer' (Q 20). God was not obligated to do this. He acted 'out of his mere good pleasure.' It was all of grace. God did not provide a Redeemer for the fallen angels. He was not required to do so for them or for us. He devised a 'covenant of grace', whereby a Redeemer and a way of redemption was provided. Why did he do this? Because he wished to do so. Nothing outside of God ever compels him to act. The impetus to save arises out of the goodness of his nature. He acts because he chooses to show mercy, a mercy that is unrequired and unobligated.

Second, salvation is accomplished through the Son. The identity of the Redeemer is established in Question 21: He is the Lord Jesus Christ. The 'eternal Son of God' who 'became man', and continues to be the God–Man, one person with two natures forever (Qs 21, 22). This 'dual nature' of Christ, given definitive formulation at Chalcedon (A.D. 451), is affirmed fully. Jesus accomplishes our redemption by fulfilling the offices of prophet, priest, and king (Qs 21–26) in his humiliation (his birth, life, death, and burial) and His exaltation (resurrection, ascension, session, and return) (Qs 27, 28). As prophet he reveals to us the will of God. As priest, he both offered himself as a sacrifice for sin and intercedes for us. As king, he subdues, rules, and defends us, and restrains and conquers his and our enemies. This three-fold office of Christ, first identified by Calvin, provides memorable categories by which to recall the totality of Christ's work. He is our prophet, priest, and king. The division between his humiliation and exaltation, in turn, provide accessible categories by which to remember the central events of Christ's ministry. Questions 20–28 are the heart of the *Catechism*, the hub around which all the contents revolve. Questions 1–19 lead up to Christ, providing the rationale for his advent, and Questions 29–107 flow from them and are built upon them, indeed are impossible without them, that is, without Christ. That is to say, the *Catechism* is not only *God*-centred, but it is also unmistakably *Christ*-centred.

Third, salvation is applied by the Holy Spirit. The great theologian of Old Princeton, B. B. Warfield, called Calvin 'the theologian of the Holy Spirit,' paralleling Calvin's contribution to that of Augustine in connection with the doctrine of grace, Anselm's in connection with the doctrine of Christ's satisfaction, and Luther's with the doctrine of justification.[2] Calvin was the first clearly and systematically to identify the Holy Spirit as the agent of application, attributing to the Spirit the role that the medieval theologians had assigned to the church. Question 29 asks,

---

[2] B. B. Warfield, *Calvin & Augustine* (Philadelphia, PA: Presbyterian & Reformed Publishing Company, 1980), pp. 485–6.

Q 29: How are we made partakers of the redemption purchased by Christ?

A: We are made partakers of the redemption purchased by Christ, by the effectual application of it to us, by His Holy Spirit.

The Holy Spirit regenerates us (Q 31), and enables the faith and repentance by which we are justified, adopted, and sanctified (Qs 32–35). All of these are unambiguously identified as expressions of 'God's free grace,' either his acts or works. By God's grace we also enjoy the benefits that accompany or flow from justification, adoption, and sanctification, such as assurance of God's love, peace, joy, and perseverance, leading to final glorification (Qs 36–38). The *Shorter Catechism* teaches that salvation is a Trinitarian project, just as did the Apostle Peter (*1 Pet.* 1:1–5) and the Apostle Paul (*Rom.* 8:12–30): the Father *plans*, the Son *accomplishes*, and the Holy Spirit *applies*. We learn from the *Catechism* that salvation, fully, completely, 'belongs to the LORD' (*Jon.* 2:9). 'Because of him (we) are in Christ Jesus' (*1 Cor.* 1:30). It is all of God and all of grace. Any system that imagines the possibility of sinners saving themselves by religious rites or moral rectitude is thoroughly refuted.

Redemption and law

Once this foundation of grace has been laid, the *Catechism* introduces the law of God (Qs 39–84). It is vital that we observe the structure of the *Catechism*. We will have more to say about this in the next chapter. For now, we remind ourselves that the law only is discussed once salvation, from election to glorification, has been completed. As we move from Question 38 to Question 39, we are led to consider the law of God in its 'third use', as a guide for Christian living. Viewed from Questions 1–38, the exposition of the law in Questions 39–81 is an elaboration of the duties of believers, of those redeemed by the Redeemer. The law has nothing to do with salvation, the layout of the *Catechism* says emphatically.

Moreover, following the explanation of the tenth commandment (Q 81), a series of questions are asked which explain that no one is able perfectly to keep the commandments and that every sin deserves the wrath and curse of God (Qs 82–84). Then the way of escape from the wrath and curse of God is identified: faith in Jesus Christ and repentance unto life (Qs 85–87). In other words, looking forward from Questions 39–81, the law is now being considered in its *second* use, as a schoolmaster that convicts us of our sin and leads us to Christ (*Rom.* 3:20; *Gal.* 3:24 KJV). What is our point? Looked at this way, *all* of Questions 1–85 are meant to lead us to repentance and faith in Christ as defined in Questions 86 and 87. We can see that the intention of the writers of the *Shorter Catechism*, revealed by their design, was to promote the conversion of covenant children. This is a gospel–driven catechism! The sustaining of the Christian life through the Word, sacraments, and prayer occupies only the last twenty questions. Certainly we are meant to go back to the law (Qs 39–84) to know our duty as Christians. Yet we are to do this only after every door that might be opened to human merit is closed by Questions 1–87, leaving only one way of escape, that of Christ Jesus.[3]

---

[3] In light of this, T. F. Torrance's claim that the *Shorter Catechism's*

The *Shorter Catechism* is not a gospel tract, as we've come to think of gospel tracts, with four easy steps to salvation. There is a place for that, but that is not what the *Shorter Catechism* is. It is profound theology. It looks at the doctrines of God, man, sin, Christ, atonement, the application of redemption, and the Christian life in depth. However, its design is the same as that of a gospel tract: to lead us to Christ. When understood with conviction and stored away in the memory, it lays a foundation for Christian service that is unsurpassed.

Section 2: A Law–Abiding Faith
(*Questions 39–84*)

We have argued that the *Shorter Catechism* is essentially a 'gospel tract,' that is, a presentation of the gospel to the children of the church. Nowhere is this more evident than in the placement of the law of God in the context of the catechism as a whole. We have argued that the catechism *first* presents the law in its 'third' use, as a guide for Christian conduct. Then, at the catechism's conclusion, it is presented in its 'second' use, as a schoolmaster or tutor, as the Apostle Paul puts it, that leads us to Christ, (*Gal.* 3:24 KJV).[4] However, whether in its third or second, it is never presented as a way of salvation; indeed, such a view is thoroughly refuted. Rather, the catechism presents the law of God as both a tool which God uses to drive us to Christ, and an instructor for those who have come

---

'detailed exposition of the Ten Commandments . . . gives it a distinctively moralistic tone,' seems misguided (*School of Faith*, xvi.)

  [4] The so–called 'first use' is a civil use, guiding society in its formulation of public laws.

to him. Let us then examine how the catechism develops those two uses.

Third Use

The question with which this large central section of the catechism is initially concerned is what we have identified as the law of God in its 'third use', that is, *duty*. Question 39 asks,

> Q 39: What is the duty which God requireth of man?
>
> A: The duty which God requireth of man, is obedience to his revealed will.

Questions 1–38 established the way of salvation. This is followed by the catechism's exposition of the Ten Commandments, including Jesus' summary of the law (Qs 40–81). The law of God is being presented in the first instance, *as the rule of life for the redeemed*. Its exposition, essentially, is an explanation of Christian duties. Here is what God requires of us. Here is what God would have us do. It provides a comprehensive explanation of our moral obligations, only exceeded in detail by the *Larger Catechism*. It outlines for us the whole Christian ethic. It teaches us our duty towards God (Qs 45–62), and our duty towards our neighbour (Qs 63–81). It provides for us and our children a short-course in worship and ethics, stimulating the kinds of moral conversations we need to be having with our children.

'Duty' is an old-fashioned word, much out of favour both in the church and the world. It was not so with previous generations.[5] There are duties which arise out of our identity as creatures of the Creator, and out of our identity as the redeemed of the Redeemer. Using some popular terminology of our day, the moral *imperatives* of Questions 39–81, are rooted in the gospel *indicatives* of Questions 1–38.

Remember, Questions 1–38 have already presented to us a transcendent and holy God (Qs 1–11), a ruined humanity (Qs 12–19), and our redemption in Christ (Qs 20–38). That which the Father *planned* and which Christ *accomplished,* is *applied* by the Holy Spirit not to those of sufficient moral purity or religious devotion, but to those who believe (Q 29). Only when the graciousness of our salvation is established fully is the law of God discussed in Questions 39–81. It is presented not as a way *to* life, but a way *of* life. It is not given that we *may* be saved but because we *are* saved. It is the rule of life *for* the redeemed not so that they *may be* redeemed (see Q 44).

The catechism presents the law of God as Jesus does in the Sermon on the Mount (*Matt.* 5–7). Jesus did not abolish the law and the prophets, but through his exposition established its proper understanding and use. The Sermon

---

[5] We are reminded of B. B. Warfield's words with respect to the duty of Sabbath-keeping. He wrote,'I am to recall your minds, it may seem somewhat brusquely, to the contemplation of the duty of the Sabbath; and to ask you to let them rest for a moment on the bald notion of authority. I do not admit that, in so doing, I am asking you to lower your eyes. Rather, I conceive myself to be inviting you to raise them; to raise them to the very pinnacle of the pinnacle. After all is said, there is no greater word than 'ought.' And there is no higher reason for keeping the Sabbath than that I ought to keep it; that I owe it to God the Lord to keep it in accordance with His command.' (John E. Meeter [ed.], *Selected Shorter Writings of Benjamin B. Warfield* [Phillipsburg, NJ: Presbyterian and Reformed Publishing Company, 1970], p. 308).

provides norms for Christian disciples. Ultimately law and grace, faith and works are not in conflict with each other. We must not let the New Testament polemic against works–righteousness distort our understanding of the proper role of God's law for the Christian. Jesus' conflict with the Pharisees (e.g. *Matt.* 23) and the Apostle Paul's with the Judaizers (e.g. Galatians) must not blind us to the positive function of the law of God. 'O how I love your law!' says the Psalmist, 'It is my meditation all the day' (*Psa.* 119:97; cf. 119:47–48, 112, 127, 163, 165). We are to delight in God's law. We are to desire it more than fine gold and find it sweeter to the taste than honey (*Psa.* 1:2, 19:10).

Reformed Protestantism has not allowed any wedge to be driven between the law of God and New Testament principles. The *Shorter Catechism* reflects this outlook. *Love* and law are not opposed, as some might imagine. The Apostle Paul defines love in terms of law in Romans 13:8–10 citing the sixth, seventh, eighth, and tenth commandments and concluding,

> Love does no wrong to a neighbour; therefore love is the fulfilling of the law.

Faith and law are not opposed. Faith and the 'works of the law' are opposed, as the Apostle Paul argues vigorously in Romans 3:20–30. The righteousness of God is manifested in the gospel apart from the works of the law through faith in Jesus Christ. This is repeated ten times in the passage. There is no mistaking his meaning. However, does salvation *sola fide* mean that the law of God has no positive function? Not at all. The Apostle concludes,

Do we then overthrow the law by this faith? By no means! On the contrary, we uphold the law (*Rom.* 3:31).

We 'uphold' or 'establish' (NASB) the law of God by faith in the sense that the law's correct and proper function is defined. No longer is it seen as the path of salvation but rather as a way of life once saved. No false dichotomy between faith and law may be posited.

Spirit and law are not opposed to each other, as still others suppose. Having established the doctrine of justification by faith alone over the course of seven chapters, the Apostle Paul in Romans argues that in Christ we have been set free from the condemnation of the law (*Rom.* 8:1–3), not so that we might ignore the law or defy the law, but,

> . . . in order that the righteous requirement of the law might be fulfilled in us, who walk not according to the flesh but according to the Spirit' (*Rom.* 8:4).

How is the 'righteous requirement' of God's law' fulfilled in us? In our walking 'according to the Spirit.' Where, then, does the Holy Spirit lead us? Into conformity with the requirements of God's moral law.

Grace and law are not in conflict with each other either. The Apostle Paul writes,

> For the grace of God has appeared, bringing salvation for all people, training us to renounce ungodliness and worldly passions, and to live self-controlled, upright, and godly lives in the present age (*Titus* 2:11–12).

The grace of God teaches the same lessons as the law of God, 'training' or 'instructing' (NASB) us 'to renounce ungodliness and worldly passions.'

We can state this rather more simply. Jesus said, 'If you love me, you will keep my commandments' (*John* 14:15; cf 14:21, 23; 15:10). There is no inherent conflict between law and grace, law and love, law and Spirit, between law and gospel. The law of God can be and has been abused. However, it need not be. Its continuing normativity means that we have eternal and unchanging moral absolutes. We have ethical standards that come to us from God and are binding until heaven and earth pass away (*Matt.* 5:18).

It is no secret that we live in an antinomian age. Worse, we live in an age of moral relativism. The problem is not just that people are lawless. Rather, our age is unique in that it denies that there is any law. The individual is left to invent his or her own 'values'. Moral standards are in the eye of the beholder. What's right is what is right *for me*. The *Shorter Catechism* is an outstanding tool in our fight against modern man's flight from God.

We may note, further, that the law of God is presented *in the fullness of its implications*. The psalmist says, 'Your commandment is exceedingly broad' (*Psa.* 119:96). The application of the Ten Commandments is not narrow and restricted, but rather, as in the Sermon on the Mount, expanded by internalizing and spiritualizing its meaning. The implications of the commandments are drawn out deftly. This is especially the case if we consult the *Larger Catechism*, which elaborates still further on the meaning of the *Shorter Catechism*. However, even on its own terms, the *Shorter Catechism* takes us beyond the negative prohibitions of the commandments to the positive principles that lie behind them. The catechism strives to teach both what Scripture explicitly says, and what 'by good and necessary consequence may be deduced from Scripture' (*Westminster Confession of Faith*, I.6).

For example, the first commandment does not merely forbid other gods, but requires that we 'know and acknowledge God to be the only true God and our God' (Q 46; cf. Qs 45–48). The second requires that we not merely avoid the worship of idols, but that we do whatever is necessary to keep 'pure and entire, all such religious worship and ordinances as God hath appointed in his Word' (Q 50; cf. Qs 49–52). The third, that we not refrain merely from vain uses of God's name, but maintain 'the holy and reverent use of God's names, titles, attributes, ordinances, Word, and works' (Q 54; Qs 53–56). The *Shorter Catechism* requires a righteousness that exceeds that of scribes and Pharisees. It requires more than mere external, formal, superficial conformity to rules (*Matt.* 5:20). It requires expansive heart obedience.

So it is that the fourth commandment requires that the whole day be sanctified by holy resting, forbids the 'careless performance' of required duties as well as 'unnecessary thought, words, or works, about our worldly employments or recreations' (Q 61; cf. Qs 57–63). The catechism is addressing our hearts, our outlook, our motives. The fifth commandment is extended beyond parents to all sources of human authority which are to be honoured (Qs 64–66). The sixth commandment guards the sanctity of human life and forbids whatever might put that life at risk (Qs 67–69). The seventh commandment guards the sanctity of marriage and requires chastity 'in heart, speech, and behaviour' (Qs 70–72). The eighth commandment requires respect for the property of others and forbids unlawful attempts to acquire wealth (Qs 73–75). The ninth commandment guards the sanctity of truth and forbids whatever is 'prejudicial to truth, or injurious to our own, or our neighbour's, good name' (Qs 76–78). The tenth commandment is understood to internalize the whole Law of God, requiring 'full contentment with our own condition, with a right and charitable frame of spirit toward our neighbour, and all that is his' (Qs 79–81).

The *Shorter Catechism* provides a format for a comprehensive review of all the duties that God requires of us touching himself, his name, his worship, and his day, and towards our neighbour, elaborated in terms of family, life, marriage, property, honesty, and heart-attitudes. It does so both comprehensively and precisely, fulfilling the old Puritan insight that we serve a precise God.

Second Use

Once the exposition of the Ten Commandments is completed, this question is asked:

Q 82: Is any man able perfectly to keep the commandments of God?

A. No mere man, since the fall, is able in this life perfectly to keep the commandments of God, but daily breaks them in thought, word, and deed.

The point of the question is obvious. *The law is not the way of salvation*. If the point was missed in Questions 1–38, it is repeated now. We break God's commandments daily 'in thought, word, and deed.' To what effect? With what consequences? Question 84 answers.

Q 84: What does every sin deserve?

44

A: Every sin deserves God's wrath and curse, both in this life, and that which is to come.

Every aberrant thought, word, or deed brings the wrath and curse upon us, both in time and eternity. Though some sins are more 'heinous' than others (Q 83), still, every single sin deserves the wrath and curse of God. The *Shorter Catechism* is now presenting the law of God in its 'second' use. Having given us a detailed exposition of our duties, it now shows us that we cannot perform our duties, and that there is resulting condemnation for each and every failure to do so. The *Shorter Catechism* does this without reducing our responsibility to fulfil our duties. It doesn't lower the bar. It doesn't have pity on us and relax the standard. It merely underscores that we have utterly failed to do what is required of us, and leaves it at that. The law of God, then, is showing us our sin and our need of a Deliverer, a Saviour to rescue us from a plight from which we have no ability to extract ourselves. 'Through the law comes knowledge of sin,' says the Apostle Paul (*Rom.* 3:20). The Apostle says of himself, 'I would not have come to know sin except through the law.' This is particularly for him the case in connection with the tenth commandment: 'For I would not have known what it is to covet if the law had not said, "You shall not covet"' (*Rom.* 7:7). All the details of the law outlined in Questions 39–81 *not only are to teach me what my Father in heaven requires of me, but are also meant to provide irrefutable proof that I can never keep that law*, that I am condemned by that law. In case the student got to Question 81 and was not already concluding, 'I can't do all that,' Questions 82–84 make our condemnation explicit. We need a Saviour to deliver us from the verdict of that law. This is exactly where questions 85–87 take us:

> Q 85: What does God require of us, that we may escape his wrath and curse, due to us for sin?

> A: To escape the wrath and curse of God, due to us for sin, God requires of us faith in Jesus Christ, repentance unto life, with the diligent use of all the outward means whereby Christ communicates to us the benefits of redemption.

Through the 'outward means' of the Word, the sacraments, and prayer (Qs 88–107), God brings us to a true 'faith in Jesus Christ' and 'repentance unto life.' Through these, faith and repentance, we may 'escape the wrath and curse of God due to us for sin.'

Law and Legalism

Not only is the law of God not the way of salvation, *the law is not legalism either*. This is not so much taught by the *Shorter Catechism* as it is implicit in its handling of law and grace, works and salvation. We could say without exaggeration that *Shorter Catechism* Questions 1–107 refute legalism. The catechism's positive teaching on redemption refutes legalism. Yet the accusation of legalism, or 'moralism' is hurled about so frequently and carelessly that it may be helpful to identify what legalism is and what it is not.

First, legalism is the attempt to be *justified by works*. 'Works' can be understood as religious duties, moral rectitude, law keeping, inherent virtue, or any other form of self-righteousness. Legalism as self-generated righteousness

46

is essentially the religion of humanity, the philosophy of all the religions of the world excepting evangelical Christianity. Jesus and the apostles aim the bulk of their polemics against works-righteousness (e.g. *Luke* 10:25–37; 15:11–32; 16:14–16; 18:9–14; *Rom.* 1–11; *Gal.* 1–5:12; *Eph.* 1–3; *Phil.* 3). Likewise the *Shorter Catechism* repeatedly and thoroughly refutes this form of legalism, as we have seen.

Second, legalism is the limiting of the requirements of the law of God to their *external requirements* without respect to internal heart attitude. The whole Sermon on the Mount takes aim at this (*Matt.* 5–7). A legalist is one who checks the box labelled murder, is self-congratulatory because he has avoided it, while he hates others or contemplates them with murderous anger. He checks the box labelled adultery, congratulates himself because he's avoided it, while indulging lust, divorce, or adultery of the heart. He keeps the *letter of the law* regarding the eighth commandment and ninth commandment while using deception and trickery to distort the truth and deprive others of their property or money in violation of the *spirit of the law* (see *Matt.* 5:21–48 cf. 23:16–22). A legalist performs all the necessary religious duties, but does so with warped motives, either to be seen by others or because of fear driven by superstition (*Matt.* 6:1–15). Legalists are 'whitewashed tombs:' beautiful on the outside but inside they are full of death and filth (*Matt.* 23:27). The *Shorter Catechism* refutes legalism with its references to reverence (Q 54), carelessness (Q 61), one's heart, speech, and behaviour (Q 71), one's thoughts, words, deeds, motives, and attitudes (Q 82). Never once do we love God with *all* our heart, mind, soul, and strength, or our neighbour as ourselves (Q 42). The *Shorter Catechism*, with the Bible, requires not the external conformity of the legalist, but the internal heart obedience of the child of God.

Third, a legalist is one whose *priorities for obedience are warped*. Granted, all of God's commands are to be obeyed. Still, there is a hierarchy of importance. Some commandments are more necessary than others. Jesus condemns the Pharisees for 'straining out a gnat and swallowing a camel,' for tithing 'mint and dill and cumin' while having 'neglected the weightier matters of the law: justice and mercy and faithfulness' (*Matt.* 23:23–24). The legalist may tithe his pennies while hating his neighbour. The legalist may keep a meticulous Sabbath, while having no mercy on the poor. The *Shorter Catechism* refutes the warping of priorities by identifying the core requirements of the Ten Commandments.

Fourth, the legalist is one who *imposes man-made rules*. Jesus condemned the Pharisees for 'the sake of (their) tradition (they) have made void the word of God' (*Matt.* 15:6). Similarly the Apostle Paul condemns the 'human precepts and teachings' which impose rules such as 'do not handle, do not taste, do not touch,' and which '[promote] self-made religion and asceticism and severity to the body' (*Col.* 2:21–23). He brands as teaching the 'teachings of demons' those who 'forbid marriage and require abstinence from foods' (*1 Tim.* 4:1–5). Those who mean to bind the consciences of believers with dietary restrictions, who elevate celibacy as an ideal, who impose fasting or sleep deprivation or other forms of asceticism that go beyond Scripture are legalists. Those who categorically forbid alcohol, dance, movies, television, and whatever else goes beyond Scripture's prohibitions are legalists. The *Shorter*

Catechism rebuts this legalistic approach by identifying what is required and forbidden, being careful not to go beyond that which is in Scripture or which 'by good and necessary consequence may be deducted from Scripture' (*Westminster Confession of Faith,* I.6). Christian liberty may not be infringed in those areas beyond the reach of Scripture (*Rom.* 14; *1 Cor.* 8; see WCF XX.). The *Shorter Catechism* is concerned with the careful and detailed application of the Law of God. However, precise obedience is not legalism. It is simply Christian discipleship.

Balance

What we see in the *Shorter Catechism* is the biblical balance respecting law and grace. Full place is given in the *Shorter Catechism* to the Law of God in both its second and third uses. It is our schoolmaster that leads us to Christ (*Gal.* 3:24 KJV). It also supplies the pattern of behaviour for the believer (*Rom.* 3:20; 8:4). We *are not* under the law as a means of justification. We *are* under the law as a rule of life. We are free from the *condemnation* of the law. We are not free from the *teachings* of the law. We enjoy Christian liberty in those things outside of the commandments. Yet we are to conform our lives to the law and prophets, to the commands of Christ, and the teaching of the apostles. Legalism is avoided by the catechism, and so also is antinomianism. We and our children are given the moral guidance that we need, yet without compromising the doctrines of grace.

Concern for comprehensive and precise obedience is not to be identified as a 'legal' outlook. Rather, it should be identified with zealous Christian discipleship. Because we love God, we love his kingdom, love his gospel, and love his law. Not only do we meditate upon it day and night, but we are eager to fulfil not *some*, not *most*, but *all* that it requires (*Psa.* 1:2ff). We do so not that we might be saved, but because we are. This is the piety of the Reformed tradition, and the teaching of the *Shorter Catechism*.

Section 3: A Dependent Faith
(*Questions 85–107*)

Jesus employs the metaphor of the 'true vine' to teach us our absolute dependence upon him for all things. We can have no life or fruitfulness unless we are united to Christ, like branches to the vine. Severed from him we wither and die. As we abide in him we have life and we bear 'much fruit.' 'Apart' from Jesus the true vine, we can do 'nothing' (*John* 15:1–5).

Similarly, the question raised by the *Shorter Catechism* at this point in its presentation is, How are those who are saved by Christ alone by grace alone through faith alone to live fruitful Christian lives? How are they to live according to the high ethical standards described in *Shorter Catechism* Questions 39–84, fulfilling the various duties that God requires of them, bearing the fruit of the Spirit in godly character (*Gal.* 5:22 ff.), and making fruitful contributions to the advancement of Christ's kingdom?

The answer of the final section of the *Shorter Catechism* is that the disciples of Christ do so by abiding in Christ through his ordained *means*, his ordinances. The question being answered by the 'doctrine of *means*', as it has been called, is, How the 'benefits' of what Christ did long ago and far away get to us here, today? How does what Jesus achieved on Calvary 2,000 years ago cross the oceans and centuries to get to us, saving and sustaining us? The answer is, God has provided *means*. What are they? Christ's ordinances, especially the Word, sacraments, and prayer (Q 88). It is to these means that the *Catechism* now directs our attention.

Means and Salvation

The placement of Questions 82–87 (underscoring that we are saved only by faith and repentance in Christ alone) between the exposition of the Law of God (Qs 39–81) and the explanation of the ordinances of God (Qs 88–107) reminds us that not only does the law *not save* (looking back to Qs 39–81), but neither do the means of grace, the ordinances, save (looking forward to Qs 88–107). We only examine the ordinances when the question of the way of salvation is answered for a second time by the catechism (first in Qs 21–38, then in Qs 85–87). It is possible, given the relentless deviancies of human nature, to place one's faith in the means and not in Christ. It is not unknown for people to talk about the Word and neglect Christ. Some may be guilty of what has been called bibliolatry. There may be sacramentalists for whom the eucharist has ceased to be a means to Christ and has become an end in itself. Consequently, the third and final section of the catechism builds on the implications of Questions 82–84 (no one is able to keep God's law perfectly and, therefore, all are under his wrath and curse) and reviews once more the *way* of salvation as a prelude to the means by which the *knowledge* of that salvation is brought to us. Through all that the *Shorter Catechism* teaches, the absolute dependence of the believer upon the grace of Christ for salvation and sanctification is maintained.

Remember Questions 1–38 are structured to take us from the doctrine of God (Qs 1–11), to a ruined humanity (Qs 12–19), to the Redeemer (Qs 20–28), to redemption (Qs 29–38). The *ordo salutis* receives careful explanation as accomplished by Christ and applied by the Holy Spirit from regeneration, to justification by faith alone, to adoption, sanctification, and glorification. After the exposition of the law and our inability to keep it (Qs 39–84), the catechism returns to salvation. How do we escape the wrath and curse of God under which the law of God has placed us?

> A 85: To escape the wrath and curse of God due to us for sin, God requires of us faith in Jesus Christ, repentance unto life, with the diligent use of all the outward means whereby Christ communicates to us the benefits of redemption.

Faith and repentance are the answer. Faith is defined as receiving and resting in Jesus Christ alone for salvation (Q 86). Repentance is described as grief and hatred of sin, turning from it to God's mercy to us in Christ, plus a 'full purpose of and endeavour after, new obedience' (Q 87). The 'diligent use of all the outward means' is added in Question 85, not as an additional qualification for salvation, but in recognition that *there is no access to the 'benefits of redemption' apart from those means*. The point is that an immediate or saving knowledge of Christ, a knowledge *not mediated* through the outward means, is *not* available to us. Some fanatical Christian sects have thought otherwise. Some Quaker groups at the time of the writing of the catechism sought a Christ not even mediated by the Word, and sought a Holy Spirit disconnected from written revelation. What are the outward means? Question 88 answers that:

> Q 88: What are the outward means whereby Christ communicates to us the benefits of redemption?
> A: The outward and ordinary means whereby Christ communicates to us the benefits of redemption, are His ordinances, especially the Word, sacraments, and prayer; all which are made effectual to the elect for salvation.

Questions 85 and 88 are saying that the Christ we trust is found in the Word, sacraments, and prayer — and nowhere else. He is to be diligently sought there and nowhere else. The Christ whom we trust and in whose name we repent *ordinarily* makes himself and his benefits known in 'outward' means. These 'outward' means are also 'ordinary', that is, not extraordinary, as in God shouting to us out of heaven. God did that once, on the Damascus road in the life of the Apostle Paul. As far as we know, that never happened again. They are 'outward' as opposed to the 'inward' means. The Holy Spirit working in our hearts is the 'inward' means. The Word, sacraments, and prayer are the 'outward' means. Another way of saying this is that the Holy Spirit changes our hearts by making use of outward and ordinary means. We are not to trust the means, but the Christ who makes himself known through the means. 'It should be our great design,' says Watson, 'not only to have the ordinances of God but the God of the ordinances.'[6] At one and the same time the *Catechism* exalts Christ as the only *Saviour*, the

[6] Watson, *A Body of Divinity*, p. 21

Holy Spirit as the *agent of application* (Qs 29, 89, 91), and the ordinances as the *only means* to either. Let's explore this scheme further.

Means and the Church

The *Catechism* envisions the Christian life not only as Christ–centred and Holy Spirit dependent, but as church–honouring as well. Among the omissions of the *Shorter Catechism* that we have identified is its failure to make explicit mention of the church (Q 95 excepted). This deficiency should be viewed in light of the more complete explanation of Christian doctrine found in the *Larger Cate-chism* and the *Confession* itself, which teaching is assumed though not stated in the *Shorter Catechism*. The *Larger Catechism* defines the visible church (*LC* Q 62) and the invisible church (*LC* Q 64). It assigns to the visible church (the church as we see it) the 'ordinary means of salvation' (*LC* Q 63). It envisions a very high view of ordination, the Word of God being preached only by those 'approved and called to that office' (*LC* Q 158). Also baptism and the Lord's Supper are both 'to be dispensed by ministers of the gospel, and by none other; and to be continued *in the church* of Christ until his Second Coming' (*LC* Q 176; cf. WCF XXVII.4). The sacraments and ordinances are 'instituted by Christ *in his church*' (*LC* Q 162; and *LC* Qs 164, 173). By baptism one is 'solemnly admitted into the visible church' (*LC* Q 165; cf. WCF XXVIII.1; and *SC* Q 95).

Beyond these high views of the prerogatives of the church and its ministry, even more emphatically, the *Westminster Confession of Faith* declares that outside of the visible church 'there is *no ordinary possibility* of *salvation*' (XXV.2;

my emphasis). To it has been given 'the ministry, oracles, ordinances of God, for the gathering and perfecting of the saints' (XXV.3). The church, through its officers, has been given 'the keys of the kingdom of heaven' (from *Matt.* 16:19), and (from *John* 20:23) the power 'to retain and remit sins; to shut that kingdom against the impenitent, both by the Word, and censures; and to open it unto penitent sinners, by the ministry of the gospel' (XXX.2).

The high ecclesiology of the Westminster Standards rejects on the one hand the overblown claims of Rome which usurp the prerogatives of Christ and the Holy Spirit, and the nearly non-existent ecclesiology of some low church Protestants in whose hands the church's relevance disappears. Rome, for whom the church is everything, and the Anabaptist tradition, for whom the church is nothing, are both wrong. This foundation is implied by the *Shorter Catechism's* teaching on the ordinary means. Salvation ordinarily is found within the church because the ordinary means of grace function primarily in the church. The church is where the word is preached. The church is where the sacraments are administered. The church is where the prayers of the assembly ('two or more') are offered and which Christ has promised to hear (*Matt.* 18:18–20). If Christ makes himself and his benefits known through the Word, sacraments and prayer, and if the word, sacraments, and prayer are primarily to be found in the church, then the church in the era of ordinary circumstances is indispensable.

Teach the catechism to your children and they will absorb a high view of the church. Today we have high profile Christians who openly admit that they rarely attend church at all. Some evangelical leaders disparage the church, and one (Barna) is calling for the abandonment and dissolution of the church altogether and its replacement by informal gatherings of Christians at coffee shops. The proliferation of para-church groups has divided the resources and loyalties of Christians, further weakening the visible church. Few understand that the church, with its ministers, officers, form of government, process of discipline, covenant of membership, ordinances and accountability, is the foundation upon which all Christian ministry rests. Destroy the visible church and the various *ad hoc*, informal, autonomous para-church ministries collapse and vanish. Few understand that the church is the primary context in which Scripture is to be read and proclaimed. Why? Because we open our Bibles first to listen to the voice of the church, its apostles and prophets, then its creeds, councils, and theologians. Only then do we speak. Humility requires it. The fifth commandment requires it. We honour our spiritual parents by listening. We read the Bible first to hear, then to reflect, finally to speak.

The *Shorter Catechism* implies, the *Larger Catechism* and *Westminster Confession of Faith* teach that the church, under Christ, should be our first commitment, first loyalty, and first priority. Why? Because outside of it, as Cyprian first said, as Calvin repeated, and as the *Westminster Standards* affirm, 'there is no ordinary possibility of salvation' (*WCF* XXV.2).

The Ordinances

We return to our introductory question.

> Q 88: What are the outward and ordinary means whereby Christ communicateth to us the benefits of redemption?

A: The outward and ordinary means whereby Christ communicateth to us the benefits of redemption are, his ordinances, especially the Word, sacraments, and prayer; all which are made effectual to the elect for salvation.

What then, are the *ordinary*, as opposed to *extraordinary* (the shout from heaven) and *outward*, as opposed to *inward* (which is wholly the work of the Holy Spirit) means that Christ uses to communicate to us his benefits.

Word

First, *the Holy Spirit uses the Word to bring to us the benefits of redemption* (Qs 89, 90). This is 'especially' the case with the preached Word.

Q 89: The Spirit of God makes the reading, but especially the preaching of the Word, an effectual means of convincing and converting sinners, and of building them up in holiness and comfort, through faith, unto salvation.

Reformed Protestantism always has held to a high view of the preached Word. Others (sacramentalists) have seen God working chiefly through the sacraments, still others (mystics) chiefly through meditation and prayer. We have held that the preaching of the Word of God is primary.

Why should I be in church? Because the Holy Spirit uses the preaching of the Word to save us ('convincing and converting sinners') and to sanctify us ('building them up in holiness and comfort'). Our counsel is, never miss church services. How do we know whether or not any given Sunday may be the one when God speaks to us and our lives are transformed? Countless Christians speak of that one sermon, or that one series of sermons, when their whole lives were changed. They were born again (*John* 3:1ff; *Rom.* 6:1ff) or their minds were renewed (*Rom.* 12:1ff). They were never the same again. 'When the fire is going out, you throw on fuel', Thomas Watson reminds us, 'so when the flame of love is going out, make use of the ordinances as sacred fuel to keep the fire of your love burning.'[7] Proper listening is addressed in Question 90 for this very reason. We are to hear the Word 'with diligence, preparation, and prayer.' We are to receive it 'with faith and love, lay it up in our hearts, and practise it in our hearts.' Never miss the services of the church. We are to position ourselves in that place where God has promised to bless. He can bless us anywhere. However, it is wise to place ourselves in those places where he has promised to bless and under those means that he has promised to use.

Sacraments

Second, *the Holy Spirit uses the sacraments to bring to us the benefits of redemption*. Questions 91–97 deal with the sacraments generally, then baptism, and finally the Lord's Supper. Through baptism we are admitted into the visible church (*LC*, Q 163). Through the Lord's Supper we are provided the 'spiritual nourishment' which sustains our 'growth in grace.' (*SC*, Q 96). The *Westminster Standards*, true to the Reformed faith, present a very high view of

---

[7] Thomas Watson, *The Ten Commandments* (1692, reprinted London: The Banner of Truth Trust, 1965), pp. 11, 12

the sacraments and their efficacy.[8] Too many, especially among some low church Protestants, have viewed them as empty ceremonies merely to be tolerated. The *Standards* see them as a means of grace, one of only three that are considered primary. They 'apply' the benefits of the new covenant (*SC*, Q 92). They 'strengthen and increase' faith 'and all other graces' (*LC*, Q 162). Baptism, though only administered once is to be 'improved by us' each time it is administered to others (*LC*, Q167).[9] Each time the Lord's Supper is administered our 'union and communion with (Christ) is confirmed,' and we 'renew (our) thankfulness and engagement to God' (*LC*, Q168). It is a covenantal meal. Consequently, as we receive the Supper we are 'renewing (our) covenant with God' (*LC*, Q174). That is, we are recommitting ourselves to Christ even as he recommits himself to us.[10] These are invaluable renewal services, the forerunners of and superior to the 'revival services' that the churches later created.[11]

[8] We think of comments of the editor of the most recent edition of Calvin's *Institutes*: 'No writer has gone beyond Calvin in his estimate of the importance of (the Lord's Supper) in the corporate life of the church' (John T. McNeill, 'Introduction' in John Calvin, *The Institutes of the Christian Religion*, Vol. 1 & 2, [Philadelphia, PA: The Westminster Press, 1960], p. lxv).

[9] On how to 'improve' our baptisms, see the classic treatment by Matthew Henry, 'Treatise on Baptism' in *The Complete Works of the Rev. Matthew Henry*, Vol. 1 (1704, 1855; Grand Rapids, MI: Baker Book House, 1979), pp. 489–566.

[10] The classic pastoral treatment of the Lord's Supper is also that of Matthew Henry, 'A Communicant's Companion' found in *The Complete Works of Matthew Henry*, Vol. 1 (1704, 1855; Grand Rapids, MI: Baker Book House, 1979), pp.284–428.

[11] See Leigh Eric Schmidt, *Holy Fairs: Scottish Communions and American Revivals in the Early Modern Record* (Princeton, NJ: Princeton

Prayer

Third, *the Holy Spirit uses prayer to bring to us the benefits of redemption*. Questions 98–107 present the *Catechism*'s exposition of prayer, especially the Lord's Prayer, in the context of the discussion of 'outward and ordinary means' of grace. Above all, this means of grace—prayer—demonstrates our dependence upon God. We cannot enter the Christian life, or grow in the Christian life, apart from the grace of Christ that is funnelled to us through the Word, sacraments and prayer. We are taught by the practice of prayer that all things, both spiritual and material, come to us by the blessing of God. By prayer we seek directly from God those things that are necessary, even our daily bread (*SC*, Q 104). If something as universal and accessible as bread comes to us only by the blessings of God, then this also is the case for everything.

The *Shorter Catechism*, we have maintained, is a gospel tract. It carries us along from God, to humanity as created and now fallen, to Christ the Redeemer and salvation (Qs 1–38). It drives home the point that we need a Saviour through its exposition of the Ten Commandments (Qs 39–81, and especially Qs 82–84). At the same time it shows us our duty as believers, reminding us a second time that we are saved only by faith in Christ (Qs 85–87). The Christian life, it teaches, is the life of those saved by the power of God and sustained by that power, as the benefits of Christ are communicated to us, not mystically, and not through the church working *ex opere operato*, but by the Holy Spirit working through the word, sacraments, and prayer.

University Press, 1989).

'He who loves God,' says Thomas Watson,

> desires to be much in his presence; he loves the ordinances; they are the glass where the glory of God is resplendent; in the ordinances we meet with him whom our souls love; we have God's smiles and whispers, and some foretastes of heaven. Such as have no desire after ordinances, have no love to God.[12]

He allows no wedge to be driven between God and the ordinances of God. 'Let it be our great care to enjoy God's sweet presence in his ordinances.'[13] Watson can at times hardly contain himself: 'Oh let this be the thing we are chiefly ambitious of,' he says, 'the enjoyment of God in his ordinances.'[14]

---

[12] Watson, *Ten Commandments*, p. 8

[13] Watson, *A Body of Divinity*, p. 21. Watson also says, 'A soul deeply in love with God desires the enjoyment of Him in His ordinances, in word, prayer, and sacraments' (*Ten Commandments*, p. 75). 'It is a great matter to enjoy God's ordinances, but to enjoy God's presence in the ordinances is that which a gracious heart aspires after' (*A Body of Divinity*, p. 22). 'The godly have, in ordinances, had such divine raptures of joy, and soul transfigurations, that they have been carried above the world, and have despised all things here below' (Ibid).

[14] Ibid.

5

PROGRAMME

How, then, are we to go about teaching the *Shorter Catechism?* What practical counsel can we provide? First, as we have noted, *parental involvement* is crucial. We would argue that the primary responsibility for catechizing the church's children falls on the parents. The church conducts classes so as to *assist parents* in the fulfilment of their responsibility. This is why the Westminster Assembly addressed 'heads of families' in its introductory statement to the Westminster documents and why Thomas Manton's (1620–1677) 'Epistle to the Reader' also is aimed at parents. 'A family is the seminary of church and State,' he argues. 'I do therefore desire, that all masters of families would first study well this work themselves, and then teach it their children and servants . . .'[1] We urge a simple and attainable

[1] *The Confession of Faith, the Larger & Shorter Catechisms* (Glasgow: Free Presbyterian Publications, 1985), p. 7, 9; also found in

goal: five minutes a day reviewing the catechism with one's children. That's all it will take for most children to master the *Shorter Catechism*—five minutes a day to review, drill, discuss, and retain. Do that, and memorization will come easily.

Second, we urge churches to conduct *catechism classes* regularly. The theological training of covenant children is both a church *and* family responsibility. Regular classes will assist the parents in fulfilling their responsibility while the church fulfils its. We have settled on a four–year cycle of catechetical instruction.[2] Every fourth year we teach the Catechisms and Confession in our Sunday School as follows:

Grades 1–4   The *Catechism for Young Children*
Grades 5–8   The *Shorter Catechism*
Grades 9–12   The *Confession of Faith*

Off years we teach the Bible systematically. But every fourth year children and youth are taught the church's doctrine through the catechisms and *Confession*. Lay people teach the youngest classes. Ordained ministers teach the *Shorter Catechism* and *Confession*. Sometimes we have started in August and completed instruction at the end of May, providing roughly nine months devoted to doctrine. Other times we have devoted a full year. This ties up our ministers in the children's Sunday School (during which hour we hold our classes) for nine months to a year. Others teach the adult classes. This is how important we think teaching the

---

T. L. Johnson, *The Family Worship Book* (Fearn, Ross-shire: Christian Focus Publications, 1998, 2003), pp. 109–112.
    [2] See page 86 for example schedule.

catechisms and *Confession* is: ordained ministers teach them.[3]

Third, we start with the *Catechism for Young Children*. From the time of the Assembly to the present it has been recognized that the *Shorter Catechism* is difficult for young children. As we have seen, a number of attempts have been made to rectify this weakness with a catechism designed for younger children (see Chapter 2). The most successful and widely used of these is the *Catechism for Young Children*. It was prepared by Mr Joseph P. Engles (1793–1861), lifelong grammar school headmaster and later publishing agent of the Presbyterian Board of Publication in Philadelphia. It was originally published in 1840 as an introduction to the *Shorter Catechism* and shows considerable borrowing from previous attempts (e.g. the Church of Scotland's *The New Catechism* of 1644, Matthew Henry's *A Plain Catechism for Children* (1703), and John Willison's *The Mother's Catechism* (1763). The *Catechism for Young Children* consists of short, even single word answers (and some longer for sure) that even the youngest children can learn. Consider its first three questions:

Q 1: Who made you?
A: God.

Q 2: What else did God make?
A: God made all things.

Q 3: Why did God make you and all things?
A: For his own glory.

---

[3] We note that Manton addresses 'ministers and parents' when he urges the training of young ones (Ibid., p. 8).

Fourth, in the classroom, we *vary the pace and approach*.

1. We *drill, drill, drill*. We go over and over and over the catechism answers. We have the boys answer. Then we have the girls answer. We divide them into teams and have teams answer. We use a chalkboard or overhead or white board. We write key words for them to see and then slowly erase them as they recite. Then we have individuals stand and recite so they get accustomed to recitation. There is no replacement for drilling. Drill, but do not *only* drill for an hour.

2. We *teach*. After ten minutes of reciting, teach. Explain what the catechism means. Show where the doctrine taught is found in the Bible. Draw out the application of the doctrine. 'What does this mean for us?' After ten to fifteen minutes of teaching, then go back to drilling. Then go back to teaching.

3. We *review*. At the beginning and end of each class session, take several minutes to review what has been memorized up to that point. As the class proceeds, this period grows longer. Review helps solidify what they have already learned.

Class time might look like this:

> 10 minutes – review
> 10 minutes – teaching
> 10 minutes – drill
> 10 minutes – teaching
> 10 minutes – drill
> 10 minutes – review

It is important that the class should 'move', that the pace and activity should vary, that instruction should bounce from one thing to another so as not to overcome the students with tedium.

4. We *ask subordinate questions*. We break up each answer by asking the meaning of each important word. This is the method behind many of the catechetical works cited above. Flavel, Vincent, and Henry, to name three, ask a series of subordinate questions in order to ensure that the meaning of the answer is understood. For example, one might ask of Question 1 of the *Shorter Catechism*, 'What do we mean by *chief*?' We mean primary or main. 'What do we mean by *end*?' We mean purpose or reason for existence. 'What do we mean by '*chief end of man*'?' We mean what is the reason or purpose for our existence as human beings. For what reason did God place us on earth?

One might ask of Question 2 of the *Shorter Catechism*, 'What do we mean by *rule*?' We mean standard or measure or even code. One might ask of Question 3, 'What do we mean by *principally*?' We mean 'mainly' or 'primarily.' Subordinate questions facilitate understanding. Memorization is rote, but it is not mindless. Spiritual value comes only with understanding. Consequently we must poke and prod to ensure that our students understand the meaning.

5. We *recite*. The field of music is one of the few remaining that still requires 'recitals'. At one time, all the academic disciplines did. Recitations were a regular part of the traditional education. The value of recitations is that they require retention at a deeper level than otherwise is the case. To be able to recall facts under the pressure of a public audience demands that those facts be deeply, even permanently embedded in the memory. We divide the catechisms into three parts. With the *Catechism for Young Children* this means roughly into groups of 50 questions. With the *Shorter Catechism* it is better suited to follow the themes within the divisions:

Recitation #1 – Qs 1–38
Recitation #2 – Qs 39–81
Recitation #3 – Qs 82–107

Each recitation must be accomplished in one sitting. To allow students to come back and recite the three questions they may have missed and then get credit for a successful recital compromises the process and lowers the memorization bar. Recitations should be word perfect and *without any prompting whatsoever*. Students should be given no help. The only exception might be when a student recites several clauses and gets stuck, the listener/judge might repeat back what the student has already successfully recited, *but no more*. Once any prompting is indulged, then a downward spiral begins of second, third, and fourth promptings which have no logical stopping point. Nip it in the bud. No prompting.

6. We *reward*. We recognize and reward those who recite successfully. The apostles did not hesitate to recognize by name those who served with excellence (see *Rom.* 16:1–16). Place the names of successful catechumens on a plaque. Give them a Bible, or a gift quality edition of the *Westminster Confession of Faith*, or a gift quality edition of Bunyan's *Pilgrim's Progress* or some other spiritual classic. Rewards help motivate young people.

Recognition and rewards run the danger of confusing what ought to be a student's highest motive, that of the first question of the *Catechism*. Still, reward is a legitimate, if not the highest motivation of our labour. Jesus used reward as motivation: 'Your reward is great in heaven' (*Matt.* 5:12). So may we.

At the same time, we are careful not to embarrass, and

especially not to humiliate those who do not successfully recite. A fine line must be walked by those in charge of the programme. Recognize and reward the achievers, yet avoid embarrassing the non–achievers.

Fifth, we plan *Sunday evening catechetical preaching*. According to Hughes Old, 'Wherever the Reformation was received, catechetical preaching was revived.'[4] More specifically, he claims, 'The Sunday afternoon or evening catechetical sermon became a characteristic of Reformed Church life through Europe.'[5] The year that our children study the catechisms, the whole church is instructed in the *Shorter* through the Sunday evening sermons.

Sixth, we *pray*. Our results over the years have been mixed. Over the past fifteen years at the Independent Presbyterian Church of Savannah we have seen twenty-seven children successfully recite the *Catechism for Young Children* and thirty-two recite the *Shorter Catechism*. We wish we had more. Even so, catechizing is not an end in itself, but a means to an end. The end is catechumens who know God and who want to serve Christ and his church. Consequently, prayer is an indispensable element in our catechizing because the effects that we wish to see in the hearts of our children can only come about through the work of the Holy Spirit. The *Catechism* itself recognizes this. As we have seen, the central role in the application of the benefits of Christ's death is assigned to the Spirit.

[4] Hughes Oliphant Old, *The Reading & Preaching of the Scriptures in the Worship of the Christian Church*, Volume 4: *The Age of the Reformation* (Grand Rapids, MI: Wm. B. Eerdmans Publishing Co., 2002), p. 17.
[5] Hughes Oliphant Old, *The Shaping of the Reformed Baptismal Rite in the Sixteenth Century* (Grand Rapids, MI: Wm. B. Eerdmans Publishing Co., 1992), p. 199.

Q 29: How are we made partakers of the redemption purchased by Christ?

A: We are made partakers of the redemption purchased by Christ, by the effectual application of it to us, by His Holy Spirit

The *Catechism* in Questions 30–35 attributes effectual calling (regeneration), faith, union with Christ, and sanctification to the work of the Spirit, Questions 86 and 87 identify faith and repentance as 'saving grace(s)' (i.e. gifts of God), and Questions 89 and 91 attribute the efficacy of the Word and sacraments to the working of the Holy Spirit. If our students are to benefit from the *Shorter Catechism* it will be only by the powerful intervention of the Spirit, empowering the Word and sacraments, regenerating them, working faith and repentance in them, and sanctifying them. Matthew Henry put it this way: 'Christ opens the understanding, and so makes the heart to burn, opens men's eyes, and causes the scales to fall from them: and so turns men from Satan to God.'[6]

Yet how does Christ do this work of enlightenment? Henry encourages parents and pastors:

> Now though Christ can give an understanding immediately, as to Paul; yet ordinarily he enlightens it, in the use of means, and gives a knowledge of divine things, by the instructions of parents and ministers; and afterwards by his Spirit and grace brings them home to the mind and conscience, delivers the soul into the mould of them, and by them works a saving change in it.[7]

[6] Henry, 'Sermon', p. 163.
[7] Ibid.

We come to faith by way of 'instituted ordinances,' he insists, '*and none is more likely to prepare for the particular applications of divine grace, than this particular application of good instruction by catechizing.*'[8]

Conversely, failure to use the means that Christ has given to his church can bear bitter fruit. Recently I received a letter from a mother lamenting her failure (and her husband's) to catechize their children, and with her lament, a plea:

> To my shame (and detriment) we never taught our children catechism, and I believe this is a huge part of the reason why they are in their wasteland abyss of a life now. Not just the learning of doctrinal points, but the *time* we could have spent with them, and them seeing how important these things were to us. What a sweet time lost . . . I want to shout it from the mountain tops, 'Parents, *please, please, please* teach your children the catechisms.'

There will be times when faithful parents will have discouraging results. There will be other times when negligent parents will have highly motivated children who will grow to both love the catechism and serve Christ. God's ways are not our ways (*Isa.* 55:8). His paths are a mystery to us (*Rom.* 11:33–36). In some cases there may be a delay between our catechetical instruction, our prayers, and the spiritual results in our children. We have noted that Thomas Carlyle (1795–1881), the greatest Scottish man of letters of the Victorian Age, turned away from his Presbyterian upbringing as a young man. Yet as he grew older he was drawn back to the faith of his youth through the catechism.

---

[8] Ibid., p. 164, my emphasis.

CATECHIZING OUR CHILDREN

Sometimes the lag between instruction and fruit in the life of the catechumen may be due to the difficulty of some of the material. Admittedly, some of the concepts of the *Catechism* are beyond the grasp of younger students, though we note that it was common in the childhood home of B. B. Warfield, the greatest of the Princeton theologians, to complete memorization of the *Shorter Catechism* during one's sixth year.[9] Robert Nassau, career medical missionary in Africa, after noting his ability to answer Dr Hodge's classroom questions in the language of the *Shorter Catechism*, explained the utility of memorizing even that which one does not fully understand:

> I thus had a reply for any one who objected to children being taught Catechism, on the ground that they could not understand it. Of course, they did not. Neither had I, in my childhood. But memorizing is easy in childhood. With that Catechism in memory it was an advantage to have its splendid 'form of words' when I reached an age at which I *could* understand them.[10]

Given our commitment to the well-ordered family, the well-ordered church, and prayer, we think that with catechizing we have the best method of indoctrinating our children, and the best hope of transmitting our faith to our children. With the *Shorter Catechism*, we say with Richard Baxter: it is 'the best Catechism (we) ever saw, a most

[9] Fred G. Zaspel, *The Theology of B. B. Warfield: A Systematic Summary* (Wheaton, IL: Crossway, 2010), 28. The source of this claim is Warfield's brother, Ethelbert.

[10] Robert Nassau, cited in David Calhoun, *History of Princeton Seminary, Volume I: Faith and Learning (1812–1868)* (Edinburgh: The Banner of Truth Trust, 1994), p. 363.

excellent sum of the Christian faith and doctrine, and a fit test to try the orthodoxy of teachers.'[11] It is an elaborate 'gospel tract' that facilitates doing that which we parents deeply aspire to do, which in Matthew Henry's words is 'to transmit, pure and entire, to those who come after [us], that good thing which is committed to [us].'[12]

[11] Cited in Schaff, *Creeds of Christendom*, p. 787.
[12] Henry, 'Sermon,' p. 165.

BIBLIOGRAPHIES & CHARTS

Bibliography of Historic Catechisms & Expositions of the *Shorter Catechism*

Baxter, Richard, *The Practical Works of Richard Baxter, Vol. IV* (19th century; repr. Ligonier, PA: Soli Deo Gloria, 1990-91).

_____, 'The Shortest Catechism', (1672), pp. 261-252.

_____, 'A Short Catechism', (1672), pp. 262-271.

_____, 'The Catechizing of Families', (1682), pp. 65-164.

_____, 'The Mother's Catechism', (1691), pp. 34-64.

*Belfrage, Henry, *A Practical Exposition of the Assembly's Shorter Catechism, exhibiting a System of Theology in a Popular Form* (Edinburgh, 2nd ed. 1834), 2 vols.

*Binning, Hugh, *The Common Principles of the Christian Religion. . . A Practical Catechism* (1671).

Boston, Thomas, *The Complete Works of the Late Rev. Thomas Boston* (1853; repr. Wheaton, IL: Richard Owen Thomas, Publishers, 1980), Vols. I & II.

_____, 'An Illustration of the Doctrines of the Christian Religion,' Vol. I, pp. 9-661.

_____, 'An Illustration of the Doctrines of the Christian Religion, Vol. II, pp. 6-645.

*Boyd, James R., D.D., *The Westminster Shorter Catechism; with Analysis, Proofs, Explanations, and Illustrative Anecdotes* (Philadelphia, PA: Presbyterian Board of Publications, 1854).

*Brown, John (Minister at Haddington from 1761 to 1787), *Easy Explication of the Assembly's Shorter Catechism* (8th ed. Edinburgh, 1812).

*Cross, Jonathan, *Illustrations of the Shorter Catechism, Proof-texts, Exposition, and Anecdotes*, 2 vols (Philadelphia, PA: Presbyterian Board of Publications, 1864).

*Fisher, James and Erskine, Ebenezer, *The Westminster Assembly's Shorter Catechism Explained by way of Questions and Answers, Parts I & II* (1765; Philadelphia, PA: Presbyterian Board of Education, n.d.).

Flavel, John, 'An Exposition of the Assembly's Shorter Catechism with Practical Inferences from Each Question,' 138-317, in *The Works of John Flavel, Vol. 6* (1820, repr. London: The Banner of Truth Trust, 1968).

*Green, Ashbel, D.D., *Lectures on the Shorter Catechism*, Vols. I & II (Philadelphia, PA: Presbyterian Board of Publications, 1841).

*Hall, Edwin D.D., *The Shorter Catechism of the Westminster Assembly, with Analysis and Scripture Proofs* (Philadelphia, PA: Presbyterian Board of Publications, 1859).

Henry, Matthew. *The Complete Works of Matthew Henry*, Vol. II (1855; repr. Grand Rapids, MI: Baker Book House, 1979).

_____, 'A Scripture Catechism in the Method of the Assembly' (1703), pp. 174-258.

_____, 'A Plain Catechism for Children' (1703), pp. 259-261.

_____, 'A Short Catechism' (1703), pp. 261-263.

*Lye, Thomas, *An Explanation of the Shorter Catechism* (London, 1676).

*Mair, Alex (d.1781), *A Brief Explication of the Assembly's Shorter Catechism* (New ed. Montrose, 1837).

*Nevin, Alfred, *Notes on the Shorter Catechism* (Philadelphia, PA: Presbyterian Board of Publishers & Sabbath School Work, 1878).

Owen, John, 'The Lesser Catechism' and 'The Greater Catechism', in *The Works of John Owen* (1850–53, repr. Edinburgh: The Banner of Truth Trust, 1965), pp. 467-469; 470-494.

*Paterson, Alex Smith, *A Concise System of Theology: being the Shorter Catechism Analyzed and Explained* (Edinburgh, 2d ed. 1844).

*Ridley, Thomas (b. 1667, d. 1734), *A Body of Divinity, Being the Substance of Lectures on the Assembly's Larger Catechism* (London, 1731-33).

Shorter Catechism (Edinburgh: The Banner of Truth Trust 'Pocket Puritan' edition, 2008).

*Steel, Robert, *The Shorter Catechism with Proofs, Analyses, & Illustrative Anecdotes* (Edinburgh & New York: T. Nelson & Sons, 1888).

The Bellefonte Series of Tracts on the Answers to the Shorter Catechism, written by numerous Presbyterian ministers, and edited by the Rev. Wm. T. Wylie (Bellefonte, PA, 1875).

The Confession of Faith, the Larger & Shorter Catechisms (Glasgow: Free Presbyterian Publications, 1985).

Vincent, Thomas, *The Shorter Catechism Explained from Scripture* (1674; repr. Edinburgh: The Banner of Truth Trust, 1980).

Watson, Thomas, *A Body of Divinity, The Ten Commandments, The Lord's Prayer* (1692; repr. London: Thw Banner of Truth Trust, 1965).

Whyte, Alexander, *An Exposition of the Shorter Catechism* (1883; repr. Fearn, Ross-shire, Scotland: Christian Focus Publications, 2004).

*Willard, Samuel, *A Body of Divinity in 260 Lectures on the Assembly's Catechism* (Boston, MA, 1726).

Williamson, G. I., *The Shorter Catechism, Vols. I & II* (Phillipsburg, NJ: Presbyterian & Reformed Publishing Co., 1970).

*Willison, John, *An Example of Plain Catechizing upon the Assembly's Shorter Catechism* (Edinburgh, 1787).

*No longer in print.

* * *

Bibliography of Studies
of the *Shorter Catechism*

Cannon, John F., 'The Influence Exerted by the Westminster Symbols upon the Individuals, the Family, and Society,' in Francis Beattie, Charles Hemphill, and Henry Escott (eds.), *Memorial Volume of the Westminster Assembly, 1647–1897* (Richmond, VA: The Presbyterian Committee of Publication, 1897).

Godfrey, W. Robert, 'The Westminster Larger Catechism,' in J. L. Carson & David W. Hall (eds.) *To Glorify & Enjoy God: A Commemoration of the 350th Anniversary of the Westminster Assembly* (Edinburgh: The Banner of Truth Trust, 1994).

Henry, Matthew, 'A Sermon Concerning the Catechizing of Youth', in *The Complete Works of the Rev. Matthew Henry in Two Volumes* (1855; repr. Grand Rapids, MI: Baker Book House, 1979), vol. II, pp. 157–173,

Hodge, A. A. & Aspinwall, J., *The System of Theology Contained in the Westminster Shorter Catechism: Opened and Explained* (New York, NY: A. C. Armstrong & Son, 1888).

Janz, Denis R., 'Catechisms', in *The Oxford Encyclopedia of the Reformation*, Volume 1, Hans J. Hillerbrand, Ed. (New York, NY: Oxford University Press, 1996).

Johnson, T. L., *The Family Worship Book* (Fearn, Ross-shire: Christian Focus Publications, 1998, 2003).

Kelly, Douglas F., 'The Westminster Shorter Catechism', in John L. Carson and David W. Hall (eds.) *To Glorify & Enjoy God: A Commemoration of the 350th Anniversary of the Westminster Assembly* (Edinburgh: The Banner of Truth Trust, 1994).

Lachman, D. C., 'Catechisms (English & Scots)' in *Dictionary of Scottish Church History & Theology* (Downers Grove, IL: InterVarsity Press, 1993).

Muller, Richard A., 'Scripture and the Westminster Confession', in Richard A. Muller and Rowland S. Ward, *Scripture & Worship: Biblical Interpretation and the Directory for Public Worship* (Phillipsburg, NJ: P&R Publishing Co., 2007).

Murray, Iain H., 'The Westminster Shorter Catechism,' in J. L. Carson & David W. Hall (eds.) *To Glorify & Enjoy God* (Edinburgh: The Banner of Truth Trust, 1994).

Old, Hughes Oliphant., *The Reading & Preaching of the Scriptures in the Worship of the Christian Church*, *Volume 4: The Age of the Reformation* (Grand Rapids, MI: Wm. B. Eerdmans Publishing Co., 2002).

_____, *The Shaping of the Reformed Baptismal Rite in the Sixteenth Century* (Grand Rapids, MI: William B. Eerdmans Publishing Co., 1992).

Torrance, Thomas F., *The School of Faith* (New York, NY: Harper & Brothers Publishers, 1959).

Packer, J. I. and Parrett, Gary A., *Grounded in the Gospel: Building Believers in the Old-Fashioned Way* (Grand Rapids, MI: Baker Books, 2010).

Robinson, William Childs, *The Christian Faith According to The Shorter Catechism* (St. Louis, MO: PCA Historical Center, http://www.pcahistory.org/index.html).

Schaff, Philip, *The Creeds of Christendom with a History and Critical Notes*, Vol. I, 'The History of Creeds' (1931, repr. Grand Rapids, MI: Baker Book House, 1985).

Strickler, Givens, 'The Nature, Value, and Specific Utility of the Catechisms', in Francis Beattie, Charles Hemphill, and Henry Escott (eds.), *Memorial Volume of the Westminster Assembly*, 1647–1897 (Richmond, VA: The Presbyterian Committee of Publication, 1897).

Warfield, B. B., 'The First Question of the Westminster Shorter Catechism', in *The Westminster Assembly & its Work* (New York, NY: Oxford University Press, 1931).

_____, 'Is the Shorter Catechism Worth While?' in John E. Meeter (ed.), *Selected Shorter Writings of Benjamin B. Warfield – vol. I*, (Phillipsburg, NJ: Presbyterian and Reformed, 1970).

Wilson, J. Lewis, 'Catechism and the Puritans', in J. I. Packer (ed.), *Puritan Papers*, Volume 4, 1965-1967 (Phillipsburg, NJ: P&R Publishing, 2004).

AN OUTLINE OF THE SHORTER CATECHISM (1)

I.   *God* (Qs 1–11)

II.   *A Ruined Humanity* (Qs 12–19)

III. *Redemption* (Qs 20–38)

     i. The Redeemer (Qs 20–28)
     ii. The Holy Spirit (the agent of application, Qs 29ff)
     iii. Redemption (Questions 30–38)

IV.   *The Christian Life* (Qs 39–107)

     i. The Law of God (Qs 38–81)
     ii. Faith & Repentance (Qs 82–87)
     iii. The Means of Grace (Qs 88–107)

AN OUTLINE OF THE SHORTER CATECHISM (2)

Section 1 | Theology | Questions 1–38

I.	Introduction & Scripture	1–3
II.	God *Attributes, Trinity, works*	4–11
III.	Christ & Atonement *Dual nature, offices, estates*	20–28
IV.	Application of Redemption *Agent (Holy Spirit), effectual call,* *faith, justification, adoption,* *sanctification & several benefits*	29–38

Section 2 | Ethics | Questions 39–81

I.	The Duty of Man	39–41
II.	The Ten Commandments	42–81

Section 3 | The Christian Life | Questions 82–107

I.	Salvation *Failure to keep commandments,* *faith, repentance*	82–87
II.	Means of Grace *Word, sacraments*	88–98
III.	Means of Grace *The Lord's Prayer*	99–107

EXAMPLE CATECHISM & CONFESSION STUDY SCHEDULE

(See page 64)

Grades*	2003-04	2005-07	Sept 2007 – Aug 2008	2009 -11	Aug 2011 – May 2012
1-2	Children's	Bible	Children's	Bible	Children's
3-4	Children's	Bible	Children's	Bible	Children's
5-6	Shorter	Bible	Shorter	Bible	Shorter
7-8	Shorter	Bible	Shorter	Bible	Shorter
9-12	WCF	Bible	WCF	Bible	WCF

Grades*	2013-15	Aug 2015 – May 2016	2017 – 19	Aug 2019 – May 2020	Aug 2023 – May 2024
1-2	Bible	Children's	Bible	Children's	Children's
3-4	Bible	Children's	Bible	Children's	Children's
5-6	Bible	Shorter	Bible	Shorter	Shorter
7-8	Bible	Bible	Bible	Shorter	Shorter
9-12	Bible	Bible	Bible	WCF	WCF

* For readers unfamiliar with the USA education grading system, grades given opposite relate roughly to the following ages:

Grade	Age in years
1	6 – 7
2	7 – 8
3	8 – 9
4	9 – 10
5	10 – 11
6	11 – 12
7	12 – 13
8	13 – 14
9	14 – 15
10	15 – 16
11	16 – 17
12	17 – 18

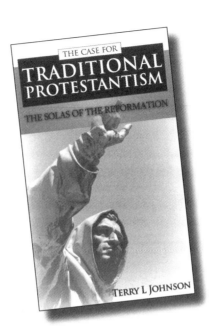

The Case for Traditional Protestantism
Terry L. Johnson

This is a timely piece of writing that argues passionately and persuasively for a serious reconsideration of the great spiritual principles that undergirded the Protestant Reformation. Far from being outdated and irrelevant to the church today, Terry Johnson shows that these very principles are the essence of biblical Christianity.

ISBN 978 0 85151 888 6 | paperback | 192 pp.

The Westminster Shorter Catechism
with Scripture Proofs

In the opinion of B. B. Warfield, the Westminster divines left to posterity not only 'the most thoroughly thought-out statement ever penned of the elements of evangelical religion' but also one which breathes 'the finest fragrance of spiritual religion'. Their most influential work, *The Shorter Catechism*, is undoubtedly still one of the best introductions to the key doctrines of the Christian faith.

ISBN 978 0 85151 265 5 | booklet | 48 pp.

— part of the *Pocket Puritans* series —